THE BLAZING INNER FIRE OF BLISS AND EMPTINESS

The material in this book is restricted. This book may be read only by those who have received a complete initiation into any highest-yoga-tantra practice.

NAROPA

THE DECHEN LING PRACTICE SERIES

THE BLAZING INNER FIRE OF BLISS AND EMPTINESS

*An Experiential Commentary on the
Practice of the Six Yogas of Naropa*

Ngulchu Dharmabhadra

Translated by David Gonsalez

Wisdom

Wisdom Publications
132 Perry Street
New York, NY 10014 USA
wisdomexperience.org

Library of Congress Cataloging-in-Publication Data
Names: Dngul-chu Dharmabhadra, 1772–1851, author. | Gonsalez, David, 1964–2014, translator.
Title: The blazing inner fire of bliss and emptiness: an experiential commentary on the practice of the six yogas of Naropa / Ngulchu Dharmabhadra; translated by David Gonsalez.
Other titles: Zab lam Nā-ro'i chos drug gi sgo nas 'khrid pa'i rim pa yid ches gsum ldan zhes bya bya ba bsdus don. English
Description: First wisdom edition. | New York : Wisdom Publications, 2024. | Series: The Dechen Ling practice series | Includes bibliographical references and index.
Identifiers: LCCN 2023043790 (print) | LCCN 2023043791 (ebook) | ISBN 9781614295440 (hardcover) | ISBN 9781614295624 (ebook)
Subjects: LCSH: Nāḍapāda. | Mahāmudrā (Tantric rite) | Yoga—Dge-lugs-pa (Sect)
Classification: LCC BQ7950.N347 D6413 2024 (print) | LCC BQ7950.N347 (ebook) | DDC 294.3/4436—dc23/eng/20231025
LC record available at https://lccn.loc.gov/2023043790
LC ebook record available at https://lccn.loc.gov/2023043791

ISBN 978-1-61429-544-0   ebook ISBN 978-1-61429-562-4
28 27 26 25 24   5 4 3 2 1

Cover and interior design by Gopa & Ted2, Inc.

Diligent efforts were made in every case to identify copyright holders of the illustrations. The author and the publisher are grateful for the use of this material. The drawings of Naropa, Ngulchu Dharmabhadra, Vajrayogini, Tsongkhapa, and Panchen Losang Chökyi Gyaltsen are © 2023 Andy Weber. The images in the color section are courtesy of Wolfgang Saumweber.

Printed on acid-free paper that meets the guidelines for permanence and durability of the Production Guidelines for Book Longevity of the Council on Library Resources.

Printed in the United States of America.

Contents

PART 3: PRAYERS AND SUPPLICATIONS

Publisher's Note to the New Edition

It is a pleasure for Wisdom Publications to bring out the *Dechen Ling Practice Series*. Ven. Losang Tsering provided a great kindness to qualified practitioners when he made available in English these incredible texts, which combine the depth of Madhyamaka philosophy with the sophistication of Vajrayana practices, as found in Lama Tsongkhapa's rich tradition.

Some time ago, I expressed to Ven. Losang Tsering that these texts had been helpful in my own practice, and this led to conversations about Dechen Ling Press collaborating with Wisdom Publications. Not long before Ven. Losang Tsering passed, we both agreed that Wisdom Publications would be an excellent place to preserve the legacy of these books and make them available to practitioners throughout the world. I am very happy to see the fruition of our intentions. May this series be a support for practitioners under the guidance of qualified teachers.

Daniel Aitken

Special Acknowledgments

DECHEN LING PRESS would like to express our heartfelt gratitude to Lama Namdrol Tulku Rinpoche and Tekchen Choling Dharma Center in Singapore for generously funding this translation project. Their great kindness will bring immense benefit to English-speaking Vajrayana practitioners far into the future and go a long way in preserving this important lineage.

Dechen Ling Press would also like to extend our deep gratitude to all the other kind supporters of these final four publications. Together we have created something truly meaningful.

Losang Tsering (David Gonsalez)
Dechen Ling Press
Translator/Director

Translator's Introduction

THIS VOLUME contains two important commentaries by Ngulchu Dharmabhadra (1772–1851). The first is a commentary on Tsongkhapa's (1357–1419) famous commentary on the Six Yogas of Naropa entitled *Endowed with the Three Inspirations.* Upon its publication, Tsongkhapa's text immediately became the basis for nearly all subsequent commentaries within the Gelug tradition, and it reflects Tsongkhapa's strict adherence to the original tantras and their commentaries composed by reliable Indian siddhas and scholars. This commentary by Ngulchu Dharmabhadra is unique in that it presents the Six Yogas on the basis of the tantric deity Vajrayogini.[1]

The Six Yogas of Naropa were transmitted to Naropa (1016–1100) by his guru Tilopa (998–1069) and were enhanced by Naropa's direct communication with the female enlightened being Vajrayogini. The Six Yogas represent the pinnacle of Vajrayana Buddhism and present numerous profound instructions for gaining access to the most subtle level of consciousness, which is used to directly realize the ultimate nature of reality. Inner fire, or *tummo,* forms the foundation of the Six Yogas and functions as the basis for transcending the limits of our conceptual minds by causing the winds to enter, abide in, and dissolve into the central channel at the navel, whereby the inner fire blazes, melts the bodhichitta substances within the central channel, transforms the mind into an extremely blissful state, and allows us to penetrate the meaning of emptiness at such a deeply profound and subtle level that enlightenment can be accomplished within

---

1. For this reason, this commentary is a perfect supplement to Pabongkha Dechen Nyingpo, *The Extremely Secret Dakini of Naropa: Vajrayogini Practice and Commentary,* trans. David Gonsalez (Somerville, MA: Wisdom Publications, 2020).

a very short period of time. Within such a subtle state, one also gains access to the extremely subtle body, which can be used for a multitude of virtuous activities. If you are not entirely successful, there are teachings on transference of consciousness (*phowa*) that allow you to transport your consciousness directly to a pure land of your choosing. For those facing a premature death who wish to remain in this world, there are teachings for projecting your consciousness into a freshly deceased corpse.

From this very brief introduction, you can see that the Six Yogas of Naropa are the pinnacle of the Buddhist sciences for attaining enlightenment. We are very fortunate to have access to such teachings, and even to merely read about such teachings places extremely powerful imprints on our minds that are certain to result in our eventual enlightenment.

I had the good fortune to receive the commentary and oral transmission of Tsongkhapa's two commentaries on the Six Yogas from my guru, Gen Lobsang Choephel (b. 1928), and have sincerely practiced his instructions to the best of my ability. I hope that this commentary will help inspire those new to the practice to receive teachings from their guru and practice under his or her guidance. For those already familiar with these teachings, I hope it will serve as an aid to deepen their understanding, appreciation, and practice.

The second text is a commentary on the First Panchen Lama, Losang Chökyi Gyaltsen's (1570–1662) *Supplication for Liberation from [Fear of] the Perilous Journey of the Intermediate State* and is a perfect supplement to the commentary on the Six Yogas. The prayer stands on its own as a beautiful literary contribution from the First Panchen Lama. It addresses the process of death, the intermediate state, and rebirth for an ordinary being in the form of a supplication to transform such frightening appearances into an enlightened experience. The text then evolves to include the nine mixings of the completion stage as the direct means of transforming our ordinary death process through the advanced yogas presented earlier in the commentary on the Six Yogas. Ngulchu Dharmabhadra's commentary is extremely lucid and concise while drawing out the subtle underlying intent of the First Panchen Lama's prayer.

The third part of this volume consists of two translations. The first is a supplication to the lineage gurus of the profound path of the Six Yogas of Naropa, based on a composition by the Seventh Dalai Lama, Kelsang

Gyatso (1708–57), with amendments made by Pabongkha Dechen Rinpoche (1878–1941). The second is the First Panchen Lama's *Supplication for Liberation from [Fear of] the Perilous Journey of the Intermediate State*, which is the basis of Ngulchu Dharmabhadra's second commentary translated here.

I offer this volume to you with a deep sense of gratitude to my gurus and the sincere hope that it will contribute to the enlightenment of all living beings.

Technical Note

This text is intended for Tibetan Buddhist practitioners who have been initiated into highest yoga tantra and under the guidance of a qualified lama. Therefore, when translating this text, footnotes and annotations have been left to an absolute minimum, being inserted only when the translator or editor felt that such amendments were necessary to properly understand the material. The titles of various texts have been translated into English, and we have provided transliterations of their Tibetan titles using the Wylie system. In this way, readers with a working knowledge of Tibetan can easily enter the transliterations into the search engine at the Buddhist Digital Resource Center and obtain copies of the texts in question.

Tibetan Buddhism in general and the Gelug tradition in particular have historically been a male-dominated religious tradition. As we enter the twenty-first century, Tibetan Buddhism is finally beginning to give women equal opportunity and access to even the most advanced teachings. Although there is still a long way to go before women truly have equality in this respect, women practitioners have taken important steps toward solidifying their rights and stature alongside men, with the full support of His Holiness the Fourteenth Dalai Lama. As a gesture of utter and enthusiastic support for the rights of women worldwide, the translator and editor thus acknowledge women in this text through the use of female pronouns. Since the original Tibetan mentions only male yogis/practitioners, the female pronoun has been added in square brackets immediately after the first use in a given paragraph of a male pronoun. (This has not been repeated each time thereafter in these spots, however, to avoid distracting from the flow of the original text.)

The outline of this text is presented exactly as it appears in the Tibetan text. Although this will not meet Western academic standards, this style is intended to be memorized and used as a teaching and meditation aid Once memorized, a practitioner can recall the entire structure of the lamrim without the need of a text. Also, when teaching, you will be able to maintain the integrity of the internal structure of the commentary without the need for a text.

Acknowledgments

First and foremost I would like to express my deep gratitude to Gen Lobsang Choephel, who kindly gave me the transmissions and commentaries to this extraordinary practice. I would also like to extend my deepest gratitude to Lama Zopa Rinpoche, Kyabje Ribur Rinpoche, Geshe Khenrab Gajam, and all my other gurus who have guided me along my spiritual path. I would like to thank Susan and David Heckerman, whose continued support allows me the opportunity to spend the entirety of my time dedicated to practice, study, translation, and teaching. I would also like to thank the members of Dechen Ling Buddhist Center who assist me in accomplishing my various activities, especially Kirk Wilson, Guru Dorje, Karolyn McKinley, Polly Trout, and others. I would like to thank the staff at the Buddhist Digital Resource Center, as well its founder, the late and great Gene Smith, for constant support in providing me with texts needed for my various projects and for the invaluable service they provide. I offer my gratitude to the late Wolfgang Saumweber for his wonderful images that serve as color inserts in this book, and to his wife, Linda, for allowing us to use Wolf's beautiful artwork. I would also like to thank my editor, Victoria R. M. Scott, for her dedication and expertise.

Losang Tsering (David Gonsalez)

A Brief Biography of Ngulchu Dharmabhadra

Ngulchu Dharmabhadra (dngul chu d+harma b+ha dra) was born in the upper region of Tsang Yä Rü Cha in the region of Rong Tö Chug Mo, during the thirteenth *rabjung*[2] in the Water Dragon Year (1772). His father was Tashi Päljor and his mother Kadro Pälkyi.

When he was eleven years old, he learned the alphabet from his elderly uncle. From then on, whenever he met someone learned, he would seize the opportunity to study the alphabet with them. As he spent most of his time tending sheep, whenever he found a flat, smooth rock or level ground, he would practice his writing using only his fingers, which would often cause them to bleed. However, this didn't discourage him. Instead, he carried on until after a short time he learned all the letters of *uchen* and *uchung*,[3] thus becoming an expert at reading and writing. Later on, the Venerable One was to become a holder of the treasury of secrets of all the conquerors. According to many scholars and pandits, it was clear that he was endowed with the characteristics of Vajradhara abiding in human form. In this respect, as it says in the twenty-fifth chapter of the *Key to the Secret Prophecies of the Great Knowledge Holder Padmasambhava*,[4]

> In a place called Je and Podong,
> Will come one with the name of Dharmabhadra,
> An emanation of Vajradhara
> Who will turn the wheel of secret mantra teachings.

2. A *rabjung* is a sixty-year cycle.
3. *Uchen* and *uchung* are two forms of Tibetan script. The latter is equivalent to *ume*, or cursive script.
4. Tib. *Rig 'dzin chen po padma 'byung gnas kyi lung bstan gsang ba'i lde mig le'u.*

Whoever has a connection with this being
Will reach the state of irreversibility
After seven rebirths.

This being of noble lineage with the name of Dharma
Was born in the area of Tsang.
Whoever at the time of death,
When all appearances of this life are setting,
Should hear the name of this being,
Will attain the state of perfect joy.

Also,

Between Eh and Dar an emanation of Vajrapani will arise
Whose name will be Dharmabhadra.

These verses clearly show Ngulchu's name and designate his birthplace as being between Podong Eh and Je Dar Ting. When still very young, whenever monks came to visit his family, they were all so surprised by his manner of thinking and acting, and by his exceptional skill at reading and writing that they could not believe he was an ordinary person. Accordingly, they were all convinced that if he were to apply himself to Dharma, he would certainly become an excellent student.

At the age of fourteen, he was admitted to Tashi Gephel Monastery. It was there that he was given the name Losang Tsering by the master Losang Gyaltsen. Early on, since he was skilled at writing, he was given one page of Ganden Lha Gyama,[5] handwritten by Khedrup Ngawang Dorje, and was told to copy it. By the sheer act of copying the text, he memorized it, and just by seeing Khedrup Ngawang Dorje's handwriting, he developed great faith and requested an audience with him. Due to his great faith, the moment he met [Khedrup Ngawang Dorje], all impure appearances immediately disappeared and he began to weep profusely. It was from this that Khedrup Ngawang Dorje recognized that Ngulchu

---

5. This is a guru yoga practice of Lama Tsongkhapa, which is translated as "One Hundred Deities of Tushita."

NGULCHU DHARMABHADRA

was a special being, and so from then on, he gave him very meaningful, heartfelt advice, and with great love he gave him copious instruction on both the sutras and tantras, like filling one vase from another. In return, [Ngulchu] protected these instructions as if they were his own eyes. He received the novice vows of individual liberation directly from the great Khedrup and was given the name Wangchuk Chösang.

From the age of eighteen to nineteen, [Ngulchu] experienced a very sad period in his life when three people very close to him—his elder brother Tadrin Wangyel, his mother, and his aunt—died, one after the other. As a result, with the permission of his lama, he went into retreat in an isolated place to practice single-pointedly, where he remained until he was twenty. After this time, he was admitted into the ranks of a *gelong*[6] and went to Ngulchu Cave, where he listened and contemplated with great effort. In the tenth month of that same year, he received the complete training as a gelong from Lopön Yeshe Päldrup, and consequently he had a lot to learn, such as how to obtain water, how to bless one's belongings, how to give and receive various small articles, and so forth. As a gelong he practiced perfectly, maintaining complete moral discipline, and so he became a great Vinaya holder.[7] From the age of twenty-two to thirty-two, he returned again and again to Tashi Lhunpo,[8] meanwhile studying with such masters as Drongtse Losang Tsultrim and Guge "Yongzin" Losang Tenzin, to name a few. In this way he studied with many learned pandits and listened to many teachings on both the common teachings and the uncommon teachings of sutra and tantra.

From the age of thirty-five on, he mainly practiced meditation but also taught extensively on the three important subjects of exposition, debate, and composition. At this time he also composed various works on sutra and tantra, which constitute six volumes of teachings. He had many disciples, such as Yangchen Drupai Dorje [1809–87], Khenchen Ngawang Nyendrak, Ripuk Tulku Losäl Tenkyong, and Dechen Tulku Losang Tsultrim, among others.

At the age of seventy, he made offerings to forty-one monasteries in Shay. Throughout his life, up to the age of eighty, he traveled to Truzin to give teachings several times; however, he spent most of his time staying in Ngulchu Cave, where he engaged solely in meditation. When he was eighty, on the eighth day of the fourth month of the Iron Pig Year (1851), for the sake of those to be subdued, he passed away into the *dharmakaya*.

In a mahamudra commentary written by Gaden Kälsöl there is a request to the [lineage lamas] that says:

---

6. The Tibetan word *gelong* (Tib. *dge slong*) is a translation of the Sanskrit word *bhikshu*, which means a fully ordained monk.
7. The Vinaya is the set of teachings concerned with the moral discipline of monks and nuns.
8. Tashi Lhunpo is a famous monastery in Shigatse, founded by the First Dalai Lama, that was later to become the seat of the Panchen Lamas.

With the skill and stability of a second conqueror,
The Protector who illuminated the Conqueror's teachings
With clear exposition,
To Jetsun Dharmabhadra, I make my request.

Colophon

Composed by Zephug Gelong Lobsang Choephel.

PART 1

Commentary on the Six Yogas of Naropa

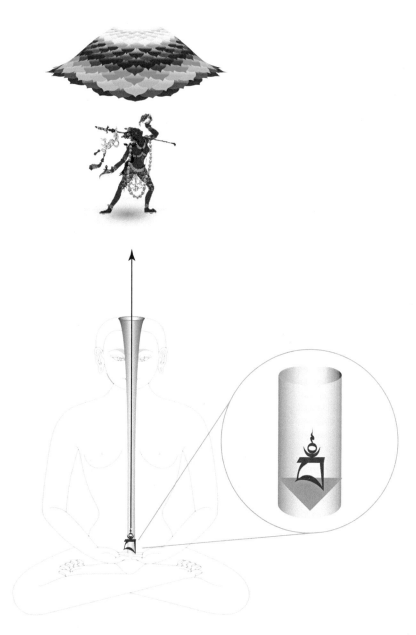

Transference of Consciousness of Venerable Vajrayogini

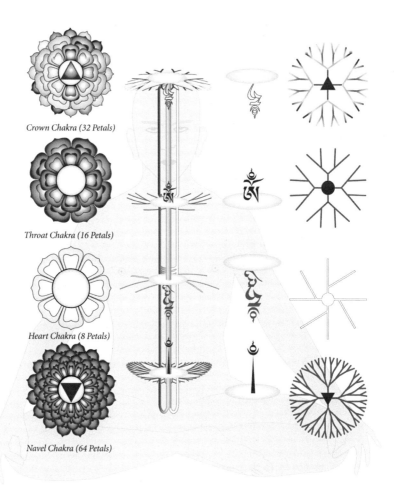

Crown Chakra (32 Petals)

Throat Chakra (16 Petals)

Heart Chakra (8 Petals)

Navel Chakra (64 Petals)

Channels, Chakras, and Syllables

Lecture Notes on the Six Yogas of Naropa Entitled "Adorning the True Intent of the [Three] Inspirations"

(Na ro chos drug gi zin bris yid ches dgongs rgyan)

NAMO GURU VAJRADHARA YA

Completely free from the extremes of existence and peace
And excellent abundance bestowing every sign of virtue,
I eternally worship the supreme guru-deity with
Incomparable kindness at the Dharma wheel at my heart.

From the womb of the spring-girl at your heart
Comes the definite goodness of union as the summer-born feast
    of the vajra, while
The cry of the cuckoo skilled in the perfect meaning of the
    Conqueror's teaching
Gains complete victory over the enemy of confusion of a hundred faults.

Your amazing song of a thousand eloquent explanations is
Like the melodious songs of the gandharva's sitar, and
Their dramatic performance of transformation reveals the meaning as
The hundred petals at the heart are uncontrollably closed.

The seals of the four channel knots arisen from ignorance
Are simultaneously released by the profound path of inner fire;
When analyzed by the tip of wisdom's finger,
The automatic result is the bliss and emptiness of ascent and descent.
The elegant form of the Six Yogas of the Siddha Naropa
Appears in a mirror as the pair of appearances and emptiness.
May my memory be unimpeded as I compose this for the sake
Of those with similar fortune who consider this with devotion
    and wonder.

*Furthermore, in order to fulfill the purpose of the incomparably kind guru, who
is the complete refuge and protector of the deities as well as migrating beings,*

our precious abbot named Jetsun [Ngulchu] Dharmabhadra Palsangpo bestowed a vast and profound oral commentary on the profound path of the Six Yogas of Naropa to his two heart disciples[9] as well as an assembly of approximately thirty faithful disciples. I was unable to memorize everything exactly as it was taught, and although I was able to assemble them in notes, I fear that this composition will fail to capture the majority of his teaching. Nevertheless, I have set out a mere portion of what was taught that I am certain comes from the lineage of teaching.

First of all, we recited the lineage guru prayer composed by Conqueror Kelsang Gyatso [the Seventh Dalai Lama], and with the exception of changing the line that states "Heruka, the Pervasive Lord of the Great Bliss Mandala . . . ," we continued with the rest of the request up to protecting the boundaries with the mantra, as done while bestowing the Vajrayogini commentary. After completing that, we recited the invocation from "Supreme Refuge and Protector . . ." up to "Buddha, Dharma, and Supreme Assembly" three times. We then recited the outline from "NAMO GURU . . ." up to "explaining the necessity of protecting the commitments" three times as we paid close attention, after which the disciples also had to recite it once on their own, after which he began:

Glorious Tsongkhapa the Great, Losang Drakpa, who appears as the guru of beings in the three realms, spoke most eloquently:

> Those who enter this path are fortunate indeed;
> With virtuous thoughts, a joyous expression,
> And a bright smiling face, listen without
> Distraction while abandoning the three faults of a vessel.

Thus you should set your motivation by abandoning the three faults of a vessel, cultivating the six recognitions, and so on.[10] In particular, you should forgo any impure perceptions of this building and instead regard

---

9. Ngulchu Dharmabhadra's two heart disciples were Yangchen Drupai Dorje and Je Trung Rinpoche Losang Tenzin (d.u.; nineteenth century).

10. The three faults of a vessel are (1) an upside-down vessel, (2) a leaky vessel, and (3) a dirty vessel. The first is analogous to not listening, the second to not retaining, and the third to having an impure motivation. The six recognitions are recognizing (1) that you are a sick person, (2) that the Dharma is the medicine, (3) that your guru is the doctor, and (4) that practicing is applying the cure; and (5) cultivating a wish for the Dharma to remain a long time; and (6) recognizing Buddha Shakyamuni as a holy being.

it as appearing as an extensive red phenomena source produced from the exalted wisdom of [Vajrayogini], Naropa's Venerable Goddess of Dakini Land, in the center of which is a lion throne, upon which sits Vajradharma as the physical manifestation of your guru's speech, while visualizing yourself as Vajrayogini. It is from within this state that you should listen to the teachings. Regarding the holy Dharma that you will be listening to, the Omniscient Je Tsongkhapa the Great stated,

> The incomparable expositions of Shakyamuni
> Are taught for the welfare of living beings.
> The foremost among these scriptures are those of highest
>   yoga tantra
> For which there are the yoga mother tantras and father tantras.
>
> The life-exertion of the short AH is based on mother tantra,
> Where penetrating the vital point of *chandali*
> As the means of actualizing the simultaneously born exalted
>   wisdom of the primordial mind
> Is primarily taught in an explicit way.
>
> In the glorious Guhyasamaja are the teachings on illusory body
>   and clear light.
> The *Four Vajra Seats [Tantra]* teaches the forceful projection.
> In dependence upon that, the supreme instructions of
> Mahasiddha Tilopa and Naropa were perfectly developed
>
> As the famed Six Dharmas of Glorious Naropa.[11]
> Limitless fortunate beings of this Land of Snows
> Have bestowed this instruction from the
> Supreme festival of the profound Vajrayana.

The foremost among all the various heaps of Dharma that were taught by our completely perfect Buddha are those of the Mahayana. Regarding

---

11. The literal translation of the Tibetan phrase *na ro chos drug* is "Six Dharmas of Naropa," but since the phrase "Six Yogas of Naropa" has become so widely assimilated in our lexicon, I use that term throughout this text.

those, there are also the causal vehicle of the perfections and the resultant secret mantra Vajrayana. Among these two, the latter [teachings] are supreme. Among those, there is a further division of the four classes of tantra, from which the very best are those of highest yoga tantra. From among those, there is also another division of the father tantra, which explicitly teaches the illusory body on the side of appearance, and the mother tantra, which explicitly teaches the factor of wisdom on the side of emptiness. Within this teaching [of the Six Yogas of Naropa] there are the vajra instructions for the path of inner fire (*tummo*),[12] and although they primarily rely upon the mother tantras of Hevajra, they also contain explanations of the illusory body (*gyulü*) and of clear light (*ösel*) that come from the father tantra of Guhyasamaja. The [Six Yogas of Naropa] also contain teachings on transference of consciousness (*phowa*) and insertion of consciousness (*grongjuk*) from the *Four Vajra Seats [Tantra]*.[13] Therefore, these instructions contain all the essential points of the completion stage of both father tantra and mother tantra, making it possible to generate all of these in your mental continuum.

The lineage came from glorious Tilopa and Naropa as the famed "Six Yogas of Glorious Naropa," and in dependence upon these very instructions, limitless fortunate beings of this Land of Snows have reached the higher states of attainment; it is these very instructions that have come down to us.

For an extensive presentation of these teachings, we use the outline of Yongzin Pandita;[14] for a concise presentation, we follow the outline of [the Second Dalai Lama] Conqueror Gendun Gyatso [1476–1542]; for a middle-length presentation of the outlines, we follow the literary commentary of Je Tsongkhapa the Great entitled *Endowed with the Three Inspirations*.[15] Although there are numerous ways of presenting the teachings, at this

---

12. Tib. *gtum mo.*

13. Tib. *rDo rje gdan bzhi.*

14. Yongzin Pandita, or tshe mchog gling yongs 'dzin sprul sku (d.u.), was the reincarnation of the famous polymath Kanchen Yeshe Gyaltsen (1713–93), who was the tutor to the Eighth Dalai Lama.

15. Tib. *Zab lam na ro'i chos drug gi sgo nas 'khrid pa'i rim pa yid ches gsum ldan zhes bya ba.* For a translation of this text, see Tsongkhapa, *Tsongkhapa's Six Yogas of Naropa*, trans. Glenn H. Mullin (Ithaca, NY: Snow Lion Publications, 1996).

time we will be following the outlines in accordance with *Endowed with the Three Inspirations*. Additionally, I will explain as much of the visualizations and so forth as I know and assemble and present the most essential points in a concise fashion.

Explaining the Precepts for the Profound Path of the Six Yogas of Naropa has two sections:

1. THE PRELIMINARY MEDITATIONS THAT ARE THE BASIS FOR THIS PATH
2. HOW TO MEDITATE UPON THIS PATH ON THAT BASIS

As has been stated, "The contents of this teaching are likened to the special milk of a snow lion being poured into an earthen vessel or a jeweled vessel. In the same way, once a disciple relies upon a special method of accomplishment as his or her preliminary..." This reveals that the preliminaries make the disciple extraordinary.

The Preliminary Meditations That Are the Basis for This Path has two sections:

1. THE INITIAL PRELIMINARIES OF THE COMMON MAHAYANA PATH
2. THE UNCOMMON PRELIMINARIES OF HIGHEST YOGA TANTRA

The Initial Preliminaries of the Common Mahayana Path

Whether entering the mantra or perfection vehicles of the Mahayana, training in the common path is a necessary preliminary. This has two sections:

1. REVEALING THE NECESSITY FOR THE DISCIPLES OF THIS TRADITION TO ALSO TRAIN THEIR MINDS IN THE COMMON PATH
2. SEQUENTIALLY TRAINING THE MIND IN THAT PATH

Revealing the Necessity for the Disciples of This Tradition to Also Train Their Minds in the Common Path

It is absolutely necessary to train our minds in the common path as a preliminary to meditating on this path. The disciples upholding the Marpa [Lotsawa (1012–97)] oral lineage, such as Tsang Rong Metön the Great of Western Tibet [Metön Tsönpo Sonam Gyaltsen (d.u.)], Ngokton Chödor of Central Tibet [Ngok Chökyi Dorje (1036–97)], Tsurton [Wangi Dorje (d.u.)] of Dol in southern Tibet, and so on, state that Hevajra is the principal deity to be relied upon for this path. These [teachers] quote the *Hevajra Tantra in Two Chapters Entitled "The Two Examinations,"*[16] which states, "First bestow the precepts..." up to "after that, teach them the view of the middle way." By quoting these sources they teach the necessity of disciples training in the common path, which is how it was explained by most of the disciples upholding the oral tradition. Furthermore, when Je Milarepa [1052–1135] was giving a commentary on *Liberation from the Perilous Journey of the Intermediate State,*[17] he stated that initially you should train in the common path—such as going for refuge, generating bodhichitta, and so forth—after which he gave the blessing of Vajrayogini and imparted the oral instructions, explaining that the terms "liberation from the perilous journey of the intermediate state" and "Six Yogas of Naropa" are synonymous. [Milarepa's] main disciple Chöje Gampopa [Sonam Rinchen (1079–1153)] also states that the common path is to be taken as the preliminary. The reason his disciple Phagmo Drukpa [Dorje Gyalpo (1110–70)] did not explain this point in his lecture notes is that their tradition is to bestow the "public discourse"[18]—which is similar to the lamrim—as a preliminary, and [this] is explained in the lecture notes of his lineage of disciples at his monastery. For these reasons, training your mind in the common path as a preliminary is of the upmost importance.

16. Tib. *brTag pa gnyis pa.*
17. Tib. *Bar do 'phrang sgrol.* See part 2 below for Ngulchu Dharmabhadra's commentary on the First Panchen Lama, Losang Chökyi Gyaltsen's *Supplication for Liberation from [Fear of] the Perilous Journey of the Intermediate State Entitled "A Hero Liberated from Fear."* The prayer itself is translated in part 3.
18. Tib. *tshogs bshad.*

Sequentially Training the Mind in That Path

You may wonder, "Well, then, how do I go about training in the common path?" According to the explanation in Jowo Atisha's [982–1084] *Lamp on the Path [to Enlightenment]*,[19] we should properly train our minds in both thought and deed in relation to a fully qualified spiritual master of the Mahayana. Therefore, in accordance with that teaching, you generate an extremely powerful desire to extract the essence of this life of leisure and endowments by considering that you only get this life of leisure and endowments this one time and it is not something you will repeatedly obtain. Once you have contemplated their rarity and great meaning, you should generate an extremely powerful wish to extract meaning from your life of leisure and endowments. Regarding the term "meaning," this indicates attaining the state of enlightenment for the welfare of living beings; however, if you have not severed your attachment to this life, it [i.e., that attachment] will obstruct your goal and you will not be able develop a strong wish to practice Dharma—and when you do, it won't last for long. Therefore, you should meditate on the Dharma teachings on death and impermanence. If you don't generate faith and conviction in the cause and effect of karma that are more than mere lip service, your activities will not become Dharma practice and you will not develop confidence in the objects of refuge. As a result, you will experience suffering by wandering in the lower realms after your death. This is how you meditate on the path of a being of small scope.[20]

You meditate on the path of a being of middling scope by contemplating that if you do not overcome your attachment to the good things of gods and men in your future lives, you will not generate a natural aversion to your attachment to samsara and your aspirations for liberation will be mere words. Therefore, once you perceive the entirety of samsara as a mass of blazing fire, you will have an extremely powerful wish for liberation and will work toward attaining the state of liberation. After that, you contemplate how all living beings in the three

---

19. Tib. *Lam sgron*.

20. A person of small scope aspires to stop rebirth in the lower realms. A person of middling scope aspires to attain liberation from samsara in general. And a person of great scope aspires to attain complete enlightenment for the welfare of all living beings.

realms have been nothing but your kind mothers; they have been kind to you in the past and they will be kind in the future, yet these kind mothers are oppressed by the suffering of samsara. Without letting this feeling dissipate, think how disappointed the buddhas and bodhisattvas would be with you, and how utterly vile it would be for you to think only of yourself while remaining in a state of bliss within the blissful sphere of nirvana. Therefore, sincerely apply yourself with great diligence to generating the mind of enlightenment based on love and compassion, and take the engaging bodhisattva vows while training in the bodhisattva's way of life through practicing the six perfections, the four ways of gathering disciples, and so forth. This procedure is clearly the intended meaning of Jowo Je [Atisha]'s oral instructions as expressed in *Lamp on the Path to Enlightenment* and of [Je Tsongkhapa Rinpoche's] great and small *Stages of the Path to Enlightenment*. Therefore, this is certainly how you should practice, while relying perfectly in both thought and deed—upon a fully qualified spiritual master who will also teach you about the great meaning and difficulty of obtaining this life of leisure and endowments.

And if through training your mind in that way you develop the wish to extract the essence of this life of leisure and endowments, [then] the supreme way to extract its essence is through entering the Mahayana, the gateway to which is bodhichitta. For that reason, you should earnestly apply yourself to the means of pacifying unfavorable conditions to generating [the mind of enlightenment]. Furthermore, dispel unfavorable conditions by turning the mind away from this life through thoughts of impermanence and so forth. Dispel unfavorable conditions by turning the mind away from samsara in its entirety by contemplating the faults of samsara. Train in the bodhisattva's way of life by generating the mind of enlightenment through meditating on love, compassion, and so forth. You should train in exact accordance with Je [Tsongkhapa's] great and small texts on the lamrim.

Je Milarepa stated,

> If you do not contemplate the purity of cause and effect
> Through virtuous and nonvirtuous actions,

The subtle ripening of cause and effect may result in
The unbearable suffering of the lower realms.
I beseech you, employ discretion and mindfulness!

If you do not observe the faults of desirable objects
And do not turn away from grasping at them from within,
You will not be liberated from the prison of samsara.
I beseech you, apply the antidote to the source of suffering
With a mind realizing the illusory nature of all things.

That was the middle scope. Furthermore,

If you do not repay the kindness of all living beings
In the six realms who have been your father and mother,
You incur the faults of deviating to the lesser vehicle.
Therefore I beseech you, train in bodhichitta
Through the force of great compassion.

The Sakyapas call this "parting from the four attachments," about which
they say,

If you have attachment to this life, you are not a Dharma
practitioner.
If you have attachment to samsara, there will be no liberation.
If you have attachment to your own welfare, you do not have
bodhichitta.
If you have attachment to grasping [at inherent existence], it is not
emptiness.[21]

The four Dharmas of Dakpo [Gampopa] state,

---

21. There are some slight differences between the original verse and Ngulchu Dharmabhadra's
paraphrase. The original composition states, "If you have attachment to this life, you are not a
Dharma practitioner / If you have attachment to samsara, you don't have renunciation / If you
have attachment to your own welfare, you do not have bodhichitta / If you have attachment to
grasping at things, you do not have the view."

> May my mind go toward the Dharma;
> May the Dharma arise as the path;
> May mistakes on the path be dispelled;
> May mistakes arise as exalted wisdom.

This is stating that you should sequentially train in the paths of small, middling, and great beings, as well as tranquil abiding and superior seeing; therefore it is absolutely essential to train your mind in the common path as a preliminary. If you practice in that way, it will prevent you from going down each path separately, and is the way of guiding you through all the essential points of the paths of both sutra and tantra in their entirety. For this reason, this system is an extraordinarily great teaching that you should come to understand.

The Uncommon Preliminaries of Highest Yoga Tantra has two sections:

1. The General Preliminaries
2. The Special Preliminaries

The reason for making the distinction between "general preliminaries" and "special preliminaries" is not that the special preliminaries are not included with the general preliminaries. All of the famed four great preliminary guides[22] are contained within protecting your commitments. As more evidence of that, the guide of going for refuge contains the verse that states "I go for refuge to the three refuges of Buddha, Dharma, and Sangha...," which is a commitment of Vairochana.[23] The guide of

22. The four great preliminary guides are (1) going for refuge and generating bodhichitta, (2) Vajrasattva meditation and recitation, (3) guru yoga, and (4) mandala offerings. See Kanchen Yeshe Gyaltsen, *Manjushri's Innermost Secret: A Profound Commentary of Oral Instructions on the Practice of Lama Chöpa*, trans. David Gonsalez (Somerville, MA: Wisdom Publications, 2019).

23. There are nineteen commitments of the five buddha families. The six commitments of Vairochana: (1–3) go for refuge to the Buddha, Dharma, and Sangha, (4) refrain from nonvirtue, (5) practice virtue, and (6) benefit others. The four commitments of Akshobya: (7) keep a vajra, (8) keep a bell, (9) generate yourself as the deity, (10) rely upon your guru. The four commitments of Ratnasambhava: (11) give material things, (12) give Dharma, (13) give fearlessness, and (14) give love. The three commitments of Amitabha: (15) rely upon the teachings of sutra, (16) rely upon the two lower classes of tantra, and (17) rely upon the two higher classes of tantra. And the two commitments of Amoghasiddhi: (18) make offerings to your guru and (19) maintain all the vows you have taken.

Vajrasattva meditation and recitation reveals the need and importance of protecting your commitments, and if they are defiled, the necessity of restoring them in general through the meditation and recitation of Vajrasattva and so forth, which is taught in the *Adorning the Essence of the Vajra Tantra*.[24] For the guide of guru yoga, the commitment of Akshobya states, "You should also maintain your gurus," [while] the guide of mandala offerings states [that you offer] "a mandala with your palms filled with flowers"—which is explained in the *Fifty Verses of Guru Devotion*[25]— and that if you offend [your guru], it is a gross infraction belonging to the first root downfall. For these reasons, in short, the four great guides of the preliminaries are included within the general preliminaries. Nevertheless, it is the practice tradition of the gurus to teach them on a separate occasion, and that is the same way I am also going to do it.[26]

The General Preliminaries has two sections:

1. REVEALING THE NECESSITY OF OBTAINING THE COMPLETE EMPOWERMENT
2. REVEALING THE NECESSITY OF PROTECTING YOUR COMMITMENTS

Revealing the Necessity of Obtaining the Complete Empowerment

At this point the outline states, "the complete empowerment," and [thus] is revealing the need to obtain the four empowerments in their entirety— which can be any of the highest yoga tantras, such as the Luipa, Ghantapa, or Krishnapada systems of Heruka, the four oral lineages of Hevajra, and so forth—yet [in any case] you must obtain the four empowerments in their entirety.[27] Regarding the four lineages of Hevajra, these are (1) the tradition of oral instruction, (2) the Dombhi tradition, (3) the Padma

---

24. Tib. *rDo rje snying po rgyan gyi rgyud*. Also known as the *Vajra Mandala Adornment Tantra*.

25. Tib. *bLa ma lnga bcu pa*.

26. Ngulchu Dharmabhadra is saying that he is not going to explain the four great preliminary guides, in keeping with the tradition of lineage gurus.

27. For more on this subject, see Pabongkha Dechen Nyingpo, *The Extremely Secret Dakini of Naropa*, pp. 22–23.

tradition, and (4) the Nagpopa tradition.[28] With respect to obtaining them in their entirety, this is also taught by the upholders of the lineage of the oral tradition who were direct disciples of Je Marpa, such as Metön [Tsönpo Sonam Gyaltsen], Ngokton [Chökyi Dorje], and so forth. Je Milarepa was the holder of [Marpa's] oral instructions, and when he met Gampopa, before giving him the commentary he asked him, "You did not tell me whether you have received an empowerment," and told him to go receive it again from Bari Lotsawa [1040–1111]. Glorious Phagmo Drukpa also said that he would bestow the commentary after first bestowing the four complete empowerments. The previous gurus who were the holders of the Marpa tradition expressed the necessity of receiving the four complete empowerments as a preliminary, which is also the true intent of the tantra. The *Drop of Mahamudra Tantra*[29] states,

> When first encountering a disciple
> Bestow the empowerment one time,
> At which point he [or she] definitely becomes a suitable
> Vessel and you can explain the great secret.

There are numerous other sources that give similar instructions.

Furthermore, if you receive empowerment into a practice such as Hevajra or Heruka, since they are related [to the Six Yogas of Naropa], they are best. If that is not possible, it is sufficient to receive the four complete empowerments of any highest-yoga-tantra deity.

Revealing the Necessity of Protecting Your Commitments

Thus, once the practitioner has perfectly obtained the empowerment and accepted the commitments of highest yoga tantra, if he [or she] doesn't even know the enumerations of root downfalls and gross infractions of that tradition, he will be without the object to protect and the act of

---

28. For a complete presentation of the Hevajra system as preserved in the Sakya lineage, see Cyrus Stearns, trans. and ed., *Taking the Result as the Path: Core Teachings of the Sakya Lamdré Tradition* (Boston: Wisdom Publications, 2006).

29. Tib. *rGyud phyag chen thig le*.

protecting; therefore, you must learn the commitments. For that there is the commitment of eating, the commitment of protecting the commitments, and the commitment of the teaching. The commitment of eating is to eat the actual five meats and five nectars, or bless your food and drink and then eat them. The commitment of protection refers to the general commitments of the five buddha families, the fourteen root downfalls, the eight secondary gross infractions, and so forth. If you have identified each of the nineteen commitments and have all four binding factors,[30] it becomes a root downfall. Furthermore, if you understand the methods for transforming them into small and middling defilements, you will go to [as] great lengths to protect yourself from a root downfall as you would [to protect] your life, and you will make every attempt to not become defiled by other faults in the first place. And although you may not think that you will be defiled, you should [nevertheless] not associate with those who have defilements and downfalls but forsake them as you would a poisonous snake that falls into your lap. You should sincerely undertake confession and restraint as quickly as possible by performing Vajrasattva and Samayavajra meditation and recitation, a Vajradaka burnt offering, and so forth. Thus, if you proceed in that way, [protecting your vows and commitments] will be included within the extraordinary four great preliminary guides, and therefore [these instructions] are extremely important.

With respect to the commitment of the teachings, this means that you should keep [with you] a vajra, bell, hand drum, counting rosary, bone ornaments, and so forth, or at the very least a drawing of them.

The Special Preliminaries has two sections:

1. PURIFYING NEGATIVE KARMA AND OBSCURATIONS THROUGH VAJRASATTVA MEDITATION AND RECITATION
2. RECEIVING BLESSING BY WORSHIPING THROUGH GURU YOGA

---

30. The four binding factors are (1) not regarding the action as wrong, (2) not wishing to abstain from the action in the future, (3) rejoicing in the action, and (4) having no sense of shame or consideration.

Purifying Negative Karma and Obscurations through Vajrasattva Meditation and Recitation

Having trained your mental continuum in the common path, as explained earlier, if you receive the four empowerments in their entirety and properly protect the commitments and vows that you accepted at the time of empowerment, that will perfectly include the special preliminaries, so there is no need to perform them separately. However, since the gurus have stated how important meditation and recitation of Vajrasattva is, some of them have presented it separately from among the four great preliminary guides, which accords with the arrangement of [Je Taranatha's (1575–1634)] exhaustive commentary *Tsembu*.[31] Furthermore, to purify your negative karma and obscurations, you must purify them in conjunction with a full set of the four opponent powers.[32] Prior to that, you go for refuge by developing faith in the Three Jewels as the object of refuge and generate bodhichitta through powerfully developing a mind wishing to attain the state of enlightenment for the welfare of living beings. In this way, think, "I am going to practice this path so that I attain the state of enlightenment." You should definitely assimilate the meaning of going for refuge and generating bodhichitta in your mental continuum, which is the power of reliance. If you are sincerely applying yourself to going for refuge and generating bodhichitta at the beginning of your generation stage, that will suffice here and you don't need to repeat it at this point. Thereafter, generate Vajrasattva Father and Mother upon a lotus and moon seat at your crown. From among the practices of the antidotes, this is relying upon the body. Reciting with special visualizations—such as reciting the hundred-syllable mantra twenty-one times and so forth—is relying upon the profound proclamation of mantra. Generating a strong mind of regret for your previous faults in general, and your faults and downfalls that are offences of your commitments in particular, is the power of destruction. The act of repeatedly cultivating the thought to refrain from your faults [in the future] is extremely important and is the power of refraining from faulty actions.

Furthermore, the *Adorning the Essence of the Vajra Tantra* states,

---

31. Tib. *tShems bu dmar khrid*. *Tsembu* means "to sew" or "to stitch two things together."
32. The four opponent powers are (1) the power of reliance, (2) the power of regret, (3) the power of the opponent force or destruction, and (4) the power of restraint.

Visualize well Vajrasattva as
The sole embodiment of all the buddhas
Abiding in the center of a white lotus and moon,
Beautified with a vajra, bell, and ornaments.
Recite the hundred syllables according to the ritual
Twenty-one times each day and your
Downfalls and so on will be blessed, whereby
They will not increase.

The supreme siddhas have explained that
You should practice during the session breaks.
If you recite it one hundred thousand times,
You will become completely pure in nature.

This is stating that if you recite the hundred-syllable mantra each and
every day, by meditating properly in accordance with the Vajrasattva ritual, you will prevent the increase of your downfalls, and if you recite it
one hundred thousand times, even your root downfalls will be completely
purified; therefore [doing so] is extremely important. You should learn
the recitation, visualization, and so forth from other commentaries.

Receiving Blessing by Worshiping through Guru Yoga has two sections:

1. MEDITATING ON THE GURU IN THE FIELD OF MERIT
2. MAKING SUPPLICATIONS AFTER PRESENTING OFFERINGS
   TO HIM

Meditating on the Guru in the Field of Merit

There is what's called "the three oral instructions when explaining nonduality." They are (1) the oral instruction for generating the guru during
the teaching of the central channel of nonduality, (2) the oral instructions
for dissolution, and (3) the oral instructions for the body mandala. For the
first, there is the "oral instruction for generating the guru," which should
be done in accordance with the explanation given during the generation stage of Vajrayogini. Nevertheless, you should meditate on Chakrasamvara with four faces and twelve arms, together with the Mother in

front of Guru Vajradharma. Furthermore, the *Five Stages*[33] of Protector Nagarjuna states,

> He is the self-arisen Bhagavan,
> Utterly one with the supreme deity,
> Because he is the perfect source of oral instructions,
> The vajra master is supreme.

This is stating that the guru is superior to even Vajradhara with respect to your personal benefit. Once you have induced absolute certainty about this, if you generate thoughts of mistaken conceptualizations about him [or her], you should repeatedly cultivate a mind of restraint. Once you examine the benefits, you should train with great devotion, through faith and recalling his kindness.

Making Supplications after Presenting Offerings to Him

The *Five Stages* states,

> You should completely forsake all [other] offerings
> And commence with perfect offerings to the guru.
> By pleasing him [or her], you will obtain the
> Supreme exalted wisdom of omniscience.

When disciples present offerings to the guru who teaches the complete, pure oral precepts, the buddhas of the ten directions come forth and enter into the body of the guru to accept your offerings, whereby the mental continuum of the disciple is purified. Although you receive merit when you focus on yourself as a buddha and so forth, it is not certain whether or not the buddhas and so forth will receive it. For that reason, from among all offerings, you should apply yourself with all your energy to making offerings to the guru. Furthermore, you initially recite the verse "By whose kindness . . ." as an offering of praise, as well as [giving] flowers and so forth

---

33. Tib. *Rim lgna*; this is Nagarjuna's famous text on the five stages of the completion stage of Guhyasamaja.

as outer offerings, and giving the inner offering of nectar. In particular, you should put a great deal of energy into accumulating merit by offering the assembly of your body as the *kusali tsok* and utilize it as a visual basis for offering the mandala. Then, make a supplication to generate the paths in your mental continuum with extremely powerful devotion for the root and lineage gurus. Next, take the four empowerments of concentration and make another extremely powerful supplication whereby the gurus are delighted, melt into light, and dissolve into your guru. These practices should be done in accordance with oral precepts.[34]

How to Meditate upon This Path on That Basis has two sections:

1. MEDITATION ON THE GENERATION STAGE
2. MEDITATION ON THE COMPLETION STAGE

Meditation on the Generation Stage

It is called "the generation stage" because you generate—or, in other words, meditate on—an aspect that is congruent with birth, death, and the intermediate state. The previous holy beings, such as the four great disciples of Lama Marpa[35] and so forth, were led through the generation stage first and subsequently led through the completion stage. The main reason you need the generation stage is to generate complete realization of the completion stage. It is the true intent of tantras that the generation stage functions to perfectly ripen your mental continuum. Furthermore, you identify the basis of purification and the purifying agent during birth, death, and the intermediate state of the time of the basis and the three bodies of the path and result, and you must have a meditation of deity yoga with all the essential points for bringing the three bodies into the path. If you also rely upon Naro Kachö Vajrayogini for your deity yoga,[36] there is a strong relationship, since both lineages [of the Six Yogas and of

---

34. Everything just described is explained in great detail in Pabongkha Dechen Nyingpo, *The Extremely Secret Dakini of Naropa.*

35. The four great disciples of Marpa Lotsawa are (1) Milarepa, (2) Ngok Chökyi Dorje, (3) Tsurton Wangi Dorje, and (4) Metön Tsönpo Sonam Gyaltsen.

36. For a complete commentary on the generation and completion stages of Vajrayogini in the lineage of Naropa, see Pabongkha Dechen Nyingpo, *The Extremely Secret Dakini of Naropa.*

Vajrayogini] come from Je Naropa. The generation stage of Naro Kachö has eleven yogas and fulfills all fourteen essential topics explained in the *Heruka Root Tantra*.[37] Once you have condensed all eleven yogas in whatever way is appropriate as a preliminary, you then train in divine pride and train in clear appearance by focusing your mind on the general and specific aspects. Next, you engage in whatever is appropriate with respect to verbal recitation and mental recitation, and perform four sessions without letting either of those two decline. Although it was not particularly clear in the previous explanations whether or not you should engage in four sessions, it would be best if you were to engage in four sessions.

Meditation on the Completion Stage has three sections:

1. THE MODE OF EXISTENCE OF THE BASIS
2. THE STAGES FOR PROGRESSING ON THE PATH
3. THE WAY OF ACTUALIZING THE RESULT

The Mode of Existence of the Basis has two sections:

1. THE MODE OF EXISTENCE OF THE MIND
2. THE MODE OF EXISTENCE OF THE BODY

The Mode of the Existence of the Mind

Furthermore, if you know the mode of existence of the basis, you will know the path. And in dependence upon practicing a path with that knowledge, you will actualize the result. With that in mind, the mode of existence of the mind in this system is slightly different than in other completion-stage systems; therefore in this system you focus on ascertaining the mode of existence of the causal basis of the object of meditation [i.e., the ultimate nature of the mind]. This is expressed in the *Hevajra Tantra in Two Chapters Entitled "The Two Examinations,"* which states,

> By nature there is no form and no perceiver
> As well as no speaker and no listener.[38]

37. A translation of the *Heruka Root Tantra* is available at wisdomexperience.org as *The Chakrasamvara Root Tantra*, trans. David Gonsalez (Somerville, MA: Wisdom Publications, 2020).
38. In Tsongkhapa's commentary it states, "As well as no sound and no hearer."

Regarding the meaning of this, it is emphasizing the ascertainment of the selflessness of phenomena and persons; therefore you should practice the view of the Prasangika Madhyamaka. Je Marpa stated,

> I went east to the banks of the Ganges River
> Where, through the kindness of Je Maitripa the Great,
> I realized the unborn nature of fundamental reality.
> I grasped the emptiness of my mind and perceived
> The essence of the primordial mind free from conceptual
>   elaborations.
> I directly encountered the mother of the three bodies
> And severed my conceptual elaborations.

Thus he discovered his view of mahamudra through his sovereign lord, Maitripa. Je Maitripa [1007–78] states, in his composition entitled *The Ten Suchnesses*,[39]

> Those who wish to understand reality
> [Realize] that it is not with aspects and not without aspect.[40]

And,

> They are merely middling [scholars], for they are not adorned
>   with the oral instructions of the Madhyamaka from the gurus.

This means that the other masters who are not adorned with the oral instructions of Guru Chandrakirti [600–650] are merely middling; therefore those [instructions] should not be practiced. However, the Madhyamaka system of glorious Chandrakirti is what you should be practicing. Je Milarepa also stated,

---

39. Tib. *De kho na nyid bcu pa.*
40. Here, the Tibetan term being translated as "aspect" is *rnam pa*, which means some characteristic that is capable of being comprehended and defined in some way; it has various translation equivalents, such as "cognitive image," "aspect," "attribute," "expression," "object," "observable quality," and so on.

To accommodate those of you with inferior intellect,
The Omniscient Buddha said,
"All things exist."
However, in terms of ultimate reality,
Nothing, from an obstructing spirit to a buddha, exists.

There is no meditator and no object of meditation,
There are no grounds to traverse and no signs of progress on the
    path,
No resultant body and no exalted wisdom.
Therefore, there is also no nirvana;
They are merely labeled by names and terms.

And,

Eh Ma! If sentient beings do not exist,
From where did buddhas of the three times come?
With no cause there can be no result;
Therefore, in terms of conventional truth,
The Buddha was quoted as saying,
"Everything in samsara and nirvana exists."

Therefore, in terms of ultimate reality, phenomena of samsara and nirvana are mere names and not inherently existent; yet, conventionally living beings attain enlightenment and so forth. Everything classified within samsara and nirvana is established through mere conceptual imputation through names and terms. This is stating that dependent arising appears as functioning things yet lacks inherent existence, and that emptiness and appearance are mutually supported by ultimate reality without forsaking one for the other. Through this we can see that the sovereign lord Maitripa, Je Marpa Lotsawa, Je Milarepa, and so forth are proponents of the Prasangika view of emptiness; therefore there is no difference whatsoever between [their view] and the view of the great Je Tsongkhapa. The completely pure system of explanation within this tradition, which is a defining characteristic of the Six Yogas of Naropa, is mahamudra, or, in other words, the view of the Prasangika.

Je Losang Chökyi Gyaltsen [The First Panchen Lama] said, "The actual practice is mahamudra, the philosophical position is mahamudra, the sutras and tantras are mahamudra, the subsequent is mahamudra, the quintessential point is mahamudra, the emergence is mahamudra, [Mahasiddha] Saraha is mahamudra, Naropa is mahamudra, the essence of practice is mahamudra, highest yoga tantra is mahamudra."

The Mode of Existence of the Body

The reason for understanding the mode of existence of the body is for the sake of understanding the essential points on which you should focus your attention. With respect to these essential points, they are the lower end of the central channel, the navel, the heart, the throat, and the crown of the head. It is [at the five places just mentioned][41] that the right and left channels wrap around the central channel to form knots, and it is from there that channel wheels branch out. It is only within the central channel, within the center of the channel wheel at each of those channel wheels, that you meditate.

Furthermore, the *Kalachakra [Tantra]* states that the lower wind is at the navel and the upper wind is at the forehead or the crown during waking. The lower wind abides at the secret place and the upper wind at the throat during sleeping and dreaming, whereby you can engage in spiritual practices, which makes them very important places at which to focus your attention. However, that doesn't mean that you can't continue with your spiritual practices by focusing your attention on those points in general while awake. In this tradition it is very important to penetrate the emanation wheel at the navel, which is the abode of the red element as the drop, or the inner Varahi.

The Stages for Progressing on the Path has two sections:

---

41. This is not to say that these are the only five places within the body where there are channel wheels along the central channel. For a detailed presentation, see Ngulchu Dharmabhadra, *The Roar of Thunder: Yamantaka Practice and Commentary*, trans. David Gonsalez (Somerville, MA: Wisdom Publications, 2021).

1. THE SIX MAGICAL WHEELS AND MEDITATING ON THE BODY
    AS AN EMPTY SHELL
2. THE SEQUENCE OF MEDITATING ON THE ACTUAL PATH

As a preliminary, you meditate on the magical wheels and the body as an empty shell, after which you progress through the actual meditations on the path.

The Six Magical Wheels and Meditating on the Body as Empty Shell has two sections:

1. HOW TO PERFORM THE PHYSICAL EXERCISES FROM THE
    FAMED SIX MAGICAL WHEELS OF NAROPA
2. MEDITATING ON THE BODY AS AN EMPTY SHELL

How to Perform the Physical Exercises from the Famed Six Magical Wheels of Naropa has six sections:

1. FILLING LIKE A VASE
2. TURNING LIKE A WHEEL
3. HOOKING LIKE A HOOK
4. RAISING THE VAJRA-BINDING MUDRA IN THE SKY AND
    CASTING IT DOWNWARD
5. STRAIGHTENING THE BODY LIKE A FEMALE DOG DRY
    HEAVING FORCEFULLY
6. SHAKING THE HEAD AND BODY AND FLEXING THE JOINTS

With respect to performing the preliminaries at this point, this means prior to the session, and Je [Tsongkhapa] states,

> Regarding the teachings that state that you should go for refuge, generate bodhichitta, and engage in guru yoga, it is definitely permissible to string them together as one session;[42] therefore you don't need to do them again. Therefore, when practicing, you should sit upon a platform for blissful meditation.

---

42. This means that if you have already performed refuge, bodhichitta, self-generation, and so forth and you are going to string together all the visualizations in the form of a scanning meditation, you don't need to stop and begin another session with going for refuge, generating bodhichitta, and so on.

For this, your cushion should be 1 cubit (18 inches) in width, square, about four finger-widths thick, the back slightly elevated, and the front section slightly lower. Alternatively, you can use a small cushion like the Kagyupas do and place a small square cushion under your buttocks.

Sit in a comfortable posture, with your spine straight, and press the thumbs of your two hands at the base of your ring fingers with your fists touching your knees. Inhale through your right nostril and look to the left. Exhale slowly through your left nostril, so that there is nothing remaining. Once again, inhale through your left nostril, and look to the right and then exhale through the right nostril, as before. Next, inhale through both nostrils, and look straight ahead and exhale once, as before. This constitutes one set of three rounds. Repeat the same process once more as before, which constitutes the second set of three. Without allowing the breath to leave from your mouth, [repeat the process once more] and complete the nine-round breathing.

(1) Filling like a Vase: For this, bend your two thumbs into your hands [to the base of your ring fingers] and take a long slow breath through your two nostrils and hold it just above the navel. Swallow some saliva without making any sound while simultaneously pressing the wind downward. After that, draw the lower winds upward to just below the navel—yet not too forcefully—and hold the [upper and lower winds] in embrace. Focus your awareness in the center of the channel wheel at the navel and hold [the winds there] for as long as it is comfortable; when you become uncomfortable, you should exhale through your two nostrils. All of the magical wheels should be done within this state [of holding the vase breath]; therefore it is nothing more than a subdivision of one of the six magical wheels.[43] When you are no longer able to restrain the wind, do not let it leave your mouth but release it slowly through your two nostrils. All the [exercises] should be done this way, without exception.

(2) Turning like a Wheel: While seated with your legs in the vajra posture, hold your right big toe with your right hand and hold your left

---

43. In other words, "Filling Like a Vase" should be practiced while performing the other five magical wheels and could have just as well been subsumed under the general structure of the magical wheels, whereby their number would have been reduced to five.

big toe with your left hand. Some traditions state that you take your ring finger and form a circle, so that your thumb and ring finger are touching while holding the breath. In our tradition, your index finger is on the back of your foot [near your heel], with the soles of the feet [touching so that they] form an open circle while you touch your thumb and ring finger. With your hands facing inward, your three extra fingers are outstretched and your thumb and ring finger hold your big toe. Keeping your waist straight and upright, circle your stomach and waist three times to the right. Then, circle [your torso] three times to the left. Next, bend your body from the left to the right, from the right to the left, from the front to the back, and from the back to the front.

(3) Hooking like a Hook: Make a vajra-fist with your two hands and cross them at your heart so that the backs are touching, and then extend them outward directly in front of yourself with great force. Then, as a preliminary, extend both [hands] to your left side with great force and pull back your right arm slowly yet with great force, as though you are pulling a bow, until it reaches your right shoulder, and [then] bend your elbow so that it strikes the side of your body under your armpit. Next, repeat it [on the other side of your body], with your left hand pulling backward to your left shoulder and striking it against your left side under your armpit. Repeat the process once more as before, with your two fists in front of your heart and outstretching them with great force. Next, extend them both to the right and pull back your left hand as before, up to your left shoulder, and then strike your side under your armpit. Next, repeat the process again on your right side as before, pulling and striking.

(4) Raising the Vajra-Binding Mudra in the Sky and Casting It Downward: Kneel on both knees with your body straight. Interlace the fingers of both hands, and with your hands like hooks, sequentially raise them upward with great force to the crown of your head. Once again, turn your hands upside-down and sequentially lower them with great force to the ground and release them.

(5) Straightening the Body like a Female Dog Dry Heaving Forcefully: Kneel on both knees with your body straight. Place both hands on the ground and place your head between them. Sequentially stretch upward with great force and straighten your body. Once again lower yourself to the ground and place your head between your hands. Turn your head to the left and right and say "HA" like a dog dry heaving. At the conclusion, rise and shake your two feet three times each. There are numerous ways of producing the "HA" that is to be verbalized, and it is said that if you expel blue water from your mouth, you are expelling the inner life-supporting wind.

(6) Shaking the Head and Body and Flexing the Joints: It states "flex the joints," for which you stand upright with your spine perfectly straight and pull on each one of your finger joints using your opposing hand, after which you massage them as though you are washing them and then shake your head and body.

Throughout these physical exercises you should restrain your energy-winds and practice them slowly and in an extremely controlled way. When you perform them, it should be before you eat. If you do them after eating, you should wait until your food is well digested and your stomach comfortable. You should do the exercises until your body has become extremely supple, with an appropriate amount of time to rest in between each one. If you do, you will prevent interferences from the outset.

Meditating on the Body as an Empty Shell

From within the clear visualization of yourself as the deity, visualize your body from the crown of your head to the tips of your toes as being a pristine vacuity of complete clarity, as though it were an inflated balloon [filled with light]. Once you focus your attention on that, you should repeatedly stabilize your meditation and alternate it with the practice of the magical wheels. You should focus primarily on carrying out these practices for a few days. This body as an empty shell is without obstruction and is similar to a rainbow. Although you are approaching this mentally, it doesn't have the capacity to actually transform your body in that way.[44]

Although these practices of meditating on the body as an empty shell and the physical exercises don't find their source in the Indian scriptures, they will prevent severe pain that may occur from forceful meditation on the channels and winds. And if some [problems] do emerge, if you are skilled in these techniques, you will be able to pacify them. These are very important oral instructions given by the gurus.

The Stages of Meditating on the Actual Path has two sections:

1. THE WAY OF STRUCTURING THE PATH
2. THE STAGES OF BEING GUIDED ON THE PATH

The Way of Structuring the Path

For this, there are two ways of proceeding: (1) meditating on the actual path, and (2) the [tantric] activities that are methods for enhancing the path. If the stages are revealed in accordance with the practitioner's capacity, there are three: those that will attain enlightenment (1) in this life, (2) in the intermediate state, and (3) through a succession of lives. There is also a tenfold division of the path in terms of: (1) the generation stage, (2) the view of emptiness, (3) inner fire, (4) karma mudra,[45] (5) illusory body, (6) clear light, (7) dream yoga, (8) intermediate state yogas, (9) transference of consciousness, and (10) forceful projection.

Regarding the structure we will be following here, it is based on the presentation above and is all incorporated within a sixfold presentation that comes from the Foremost Great Being [Tsongkhapa], who structured them as: (1) & (2) the inner fire and karma mudra taught in the *Hevajra Tantra*, (3) & (4) the illusory body and clear light taught in the Arya tradition of Guhyasamaja, and (5) & (6) the transference of consciousness and insertion of consciousness taught in the *Four Vajra Seats*

---

44. This means that this meditation does not have the capacity to actually transform your physical body into the nature of unobstructed light.

45. A karma mudra is a physical consort. The Tibetan term *las* is a translation of the Sanskrit word "karma," which is intended to indicate that such a consort is a human being born through the force of karma.

Tantra. Because they rely on these three sources, [Tsongkhapa] entitled his treatise *Endowed with the Three Inspirations.*[46] Regarding Je [Tsongkhapa's] position in presenting the Six Yogas, he lists them as (1) inner fire, (2) karma mudra, (3) illusory body, (4) clear light, (5) transference of consciousness, and (6) forceful projection.

In general, prior to [the actual meditations on] the stage of completion of highest yoga tantra, it is indispensable that there be a special method for bringing the winds of the right and left channels into the central channel, and there are a multitude of tantras and traditions of the mahasiddhas for accomplishing that. However, in this instance we utilize pranayama[47] of the short AH of inner fire in dependence upon the emanation wheel at the navel. It for this reason that Je Milarepa said to Gampopa,

> Just as you won't get oil by crushing sand, [so]
> Your system of concentration is insufficient;
> You should meditate on the pranayama
> Of the short AH of inner fire.

In the initial stages of the completion stage, you bring the winds into the central channel, whereby you generate simultaneously born great bliss, which is the basis upon which the other stages of completion are based. You should understand that because of this process, we have the well-known tradition of proclaiming that "inner fire is the cornerstone of the path."

The Stages of Being Guided on the Path has two sections:

46. Tib. *Yid ches gsum ldan.* From this perspective, an alternate translation would be *Endowed with the Three Reliable Sources.*

47. The Sanskrit translation equivalent for the Tibetan term *srog rtsol* is "pranayama," which can be accurately translated as "vitality and exertion." However, this translation doesn't properly convey the meaning of either component of the term. Like the original Sanskrit term, the Tibetan translation equivalent contains two words, *srog* and *rtsol.* The first word, *srog,* refers to our life force, which operates in the form of a subtle energy-wind that sustains our life. The term *rtsol* is more troublesome; it literally means "exertion" but more specifically refers to controlling and restraining the flow of our life-supporting wind (*srog*) as a means of gaining spiritual insights through practice of the completion stage. It also serves a secondary purpose of extending our lifespan since the *srog* is the foundation of our vitality and life force. Due to these considerations, I revert to the original Sanskrit term "pranayama" in this work.

1. THE MEANING OF BEING GUIDED ALONG THE PATH
2. HOW TO PERFORM THE TANTRIC ACTIVITIES FOR ENHANCING THE PATH

The Meaning of Being Guided along the Path has two sections:

1. THE MEANING OF THE ACTUAL PATH
2. TRANSFERENCE OF CONSCIOUSNESS AND INSERTION OF CONSCIOUSNESS AS THE LIMBS OF THE PATH

The Meaning of the Actual Path has two sections:

1. GENERATING THE FOUR JOYS BY DRAWING THE WINDS INTO THE CENTRAL CHANNEL
2. HOW TO MEDITATE ON THE ILLUSORY BODY AND THE CLEAR LIGHT IN DEPENDENCE UPON THAT

Generating the Four Joys by Drawing the Winds into the Central Channel has two sections:

1. MEDITATING ON THE INNER CONDITION OF INNER FIRE
2. RELYING UPON THE OUTER CONDITION OF A KARMA MUDRA

Meditating on the Inner Condition of Inner Fire has two sections:

1. ABSORBING THE WINDS INTO THE CENTRAL CHANNEL THROUGH MEDITATION ON INNER FIRE
2. HOW TO GENERATE THE FOUR JOYS IN DEPENDENCE UPON COLLECTING [THE WINDS]

Absorbing the Winds into the Central Channel through Meditation on Inner Fire has two sections:

1. HOW TO MEDITATE ON INNER FIRE
2. HOW TO CAUSE THE WINDS TO ENTER, ABIDE IN, AND DISSOLVE INTO THE CENTRAL CHANNEL THROUGH MEDITATING IN THIS WAY

How to Meditate on Inner Fire has three sections:

1. Meditation through Visualizing the Channels
2. Meditation through Visualizing the Syllables
3. How to Meditate on the Vase Breathing of Wind

Meditation through Visualizing the Channels

According to Je [Tsongkhapa's] commentary, you should meditate on guru yoga and make supplications, as explained earlier, as a general preliminary. However, if you have already done this, you don't need to do it again at this point. As explained before, sit upon a comfortable seat with your legs bound in with a meditation belt, with either your right or left leg in the inner or outer position; it doesn't matter which way. You bind your thighs so that your knees are raised. The color of your meditation belt should correspond to the color of the deity you are generating [yourself] as. It should be six finger-widths wide or, alternatively, the width of your fist with your thumb placed on top. Its length should be such that by folding it in two and wrapping it around the nape of your neck, the tips almost meet at your forehead. The system for wearing it is to tie it around your waist and two knees.

Your spine should be straight, your neck slightly bent, your eyes gazing toward the tip of your nose, your tongue touching your palate, your lips and teeth relaxed in their natural position, and your hands in the mudra of meditative equipoise placed just below your navel or, alternatively, in the "six hearths" posture.[48] For this posture, your two hands are crossed in front of your [chest] with your fingers touching the tops of your shoulders, and your two elbows are set upon your two knees; in this way the six [triangular] phenomena sources are formed. This is also called "binding the sealing knot."

Having your body and mind on slightly heightened alert and your body generated in the image of a hollow body are the essential features of a body that has a dependent relationship for quickly generating bliss and warmth. It is excellent if you prepare with the six magical wheels, which will be effective in clearing the stale winds. If you don't [perform the six

---

48. Tib. *me thab drug*, which means "six fire hearths," so named because in this instance, a hearth is triangular, and when sitting with a meditation belt, one's limbs form the shape of six triangles.

magical wheels], you should meditate on clearing the stale winds as well as meditating on the hollow body as an empty shell. Regarding the essential point of time, this refers to dawn, when your awareness is clear, and the afternoon, which is the best time for generating inner fire.

Regarding the essential point of visual reference, visualize your central channel in the center of your body and a little closer to your spine. The central channel is blue. Its lower end reaches four finger-widths below the navel and the upper end terminates at the crown of your head. While performing vase breathing, [the central channel] goes to the crown of your head, bends, and terminates between your eyebrows. It is straight, soft, in the aspect of being full,[49] and has the diameter of a wheat straw. To the right is the red "roma" channel and to the left is the white "kyangma" channel. These two are the diameter of a middling wheat straw and in the aspect of being slightly deflated. Their upper ends terminate at the two nostrils and their lower ends curve into and enter the central channel like a Tibetan syllable CHA.

At the time of the basis,[50] there are knots at the navel, heart, throat, and crown that are formed by the right and left channels. However, during meditation, regardless of whether or not you meditate on the knots, it is permissible to condense the visualization into a single vacuole formed by the three channels at each of the channel knots.

With respect to the channel wheels, four channel petals branch out in the [four] cardinal directions from the emanation wheel at the navel. Channels branch out from each of those, forming eight. Channels branch out from each of those, forming sixteen. Four channels branch out from each one of those, forming sixty-four. They are red in color. Their outer shape is triangular like the syllable E, and they rise upward like an upright umbrella.

49. Generally, the winds are not flowing through the central channel; therefore, for auspiciousness, you imagine that it is full of energy-winds while imagining the right and left channels to be deflated.
50. This is as opposed to during the path and the result.

Four channel petals branch out in the four cardinal directions from the Dharma wheel at the heart. Channels branch out from each one of those in the four intermediate directions, forming eight. They are white in color. Their outer shape is round like the syllable VAM, and they face downward.

Four channel petals branch out in the [four] cardinal directions from the wheel of enjoyment at your throat. Channels branch out from each one of those, forming eight. Channels branch out from each one of those, forming sixteen. They are red in color. Their outer shape is round like a syllable VAM, and they face upward.

Four channel petals branch out in the four cardinal directions from the wheel of great bliss at the crown. Channels branch out from each one of those, forming eight. Channels branch out from each one of those, forming sixteen. Channels branch out from each one of those, forming thirty-two. They are various colors. Their outer shape is like the syllable E, and they face downward.

In this way, the channels are paired in the manner of conjoining method and wisdom.[51] Once you have visualized the channels in this way, you should elicit clear appearance. From the outset, you should not focus your attention for more than a short time on the upper three channel wheels; otherwise there is a danger of creating obstacles.[52] Therefore, you should meditate by focusing your attention primarily in the center of the channel wheel at your navel. Other sources explain training in the pathway of the channels; therefore, it is permissible to practice training in the pathway of the channels at this point. However, Je [Rinpoche's] text does not teach it, so it is permissible not to practice it as well.[53]

51. The four channels are grouped into two pairs and are facing each other, so that their shapes are represented by E and VAM, respectively. The fact that they are facing each other symbolizes the union of EVAM as that of method and wisdom. For a detailed explanation of the meaning of EVAM, see Kyabje Trijang Rinpoche Losang Yeshe, *The Ecstatic Dance of Chakrasamvara: Heruka Body Mandala Practice and Commentary* (Seattle: Dechen Ling Press, 2013).

52. Since you are attempting to bring the winds into the navel channel wheel, if you focus for too long on the other channel wheels, it can draw your attention away from the navel channel wheel.

53. Ngulchu Dharmabhadra's *Roar of Thunder* states, "Concerning this, within your central channel at your heart is a white drop the size of a pea with a red luster that is inseparable from your three doors and the three secrets of the guru and deity. It is as if your mind has entered into it. From the front of the channel wheel, you can see what the channel petals are like to the right and left. The central channel is completely hollow and unobstructed, such that you can see the

Meditation through Visualizing the Syllables

It is important to meditate on the syllables at all four channel wheels, for which there are both extensive and concise systems of meditation. Here I shall present the concise system. Furthermore, within the central channel, in the center of the channel wheel at the navel is a moon seat, described as being the size of a split pea cut in half. A split pea is a type of pea; therefore the moon seat is the size of a small pea cut in half, in the center of which is a short AH in the Sanskrit alphabet, which corresponds roughly to a division stroke in Tibetan block writing[54] and is like a thorn of a barberry plant. It is red in color and is standing upright upon the moon seat, and it is topped off with a crescent moon and so forth.

Within the central channel at your heart channel wheel is a blue inverted HUM hanging from a moon seat. It is like a pillar of bodhichitta that is on the verge of dripping. In the center of the channel wheel at your throat is a red upright OM upon a moon seat. In the center of the channel wheel at your crown is an inverted white HAM hanging from a moon cushion. The right and left channels form knots by wrapping around the central channel at each of the channel wheels. Within the central chan-

---

channel wheel of the navel. Again, look upward through the channel wheel at the throat and travel with ease upward within the central channel. You remain in the center of the channel wheel for a short time and examine the channels as before. You travel upward, remain in the center of the channel wheel at the crown briefly, and examine [the channel wheel] as before. You look at the opening between the eyes, and having gone there, half of the drop protrudes from the upper opening [of the central channel] illuminating and observing the infinite purity of the world and its beings as well as your utter and complete purity as the deity. You once again return through the pathway of the central channel and examine the crown, throat, and heart channel wheels as before. Looking downward at the navel channel wheel, you travel there with ease. You examine the channel petals as before. In the same way, you go to the secret place and the channel wheel at the jewel and examine them. [Half of the drop] protrudes from the tip of the sex organ, and you examine [everything] as before. Sequentially travel upward again to the jewel, secret place, and navel channel wheels while examining the channel petals to the right and left. You should repeatedly travel up and down through the central channel in that way, going from the upper end to the lower end. If you wish to end the session, you should recite either extensive or concise dedication prayers. It is taught that through combining the practices of the training in the pathway of the channels for a few days, you will obtain signs in dreams, such as emerging from a cave and so forth; therefore, you should continue training until such signs occur" (181–82).

54. The short AH looks like a toothpick standing upright, which is very similar to a *shad* (or division stroke) in Tibetan block letters.

nel, at the exact center of each channel wheel, [are the syllables]. They are the circumference of mustard seeds and have a crescent moon, drop, and *nada*. It is very important that you meditate on all three upper syllables as being in the aspect of dewdrops that are on the verge of dripping. If you meditate on them being like melting dewdrops, you will have a very blissful experience, and if you visualize the syllables as being radiant and very brilliant, you will easily eliminate mental sinking and [have] a very clear experience of concentration. You should not view them as being separate from your mind, as though appearing from their own side. Instead, you should sink your subjective mind into the object and blend your mind with them. Once you develop the experience of your mind being utterly mixed with the drop, it will be very easy to collect the winds into that place. Furthermore, you should focus your attention predominantly on the short AH and the other syllables for just a short time.

If in the beginning, it is difficult to visualize such a subtle object, you can make it slightly larger and then focus on a subtle object once you gain stability.

How to Meditate on the Vase Breathing of Wind

Thus, there are channel wheels, and in the center of those four channel wheels are syllables. In particular, because of the essential point of the wind and mind being a single engager,[55] if you gain a factor of stability by focusing the mind on the short AH at the channel wheel of the navel, your mind will absorb and collect where it is focused. Although meditating on vase breathing at this point is not taught in tantras and Indian texts, the Tibetan lamas have created a combination of meditating on inner fire and on vase breathing. With respect to [this latter system], it is performed for the sake of quickly generating an experience of inner fire. For that, they

---

55. The term "single engager" means that the wind and mind function together and are often likened to a horse and its rider: wherever rider-like mind focuses its attention, the horse-like winds will travel as well. Because they function together in this way and are interdependent, they are referred to as "a single engager." For this reason, success in drawing the winds into the central channel is almost entirely dependent upon the ability of the mind to focus on an object within the central channel.

have explained a system for practicing that contains four stages: (1) inhaling, (2) holding, (3) expelling, and (4) releasing like an arrow.

Regarding the essential point of time, it is stated that you should commence your meditation when the upward-moving wind called the vajra lotus protector is primarily functioning. Regarding this, this is when the shepherds are leaving to herd their sheep and when the roosters are crowing.[56]

Regarding **inhaling**, you don't inhale through your mouth; instead take a slow, long, and gentle inhalation through your two nostrils without force. With respect to **holding**, without exhaling between inhalations, compress the winds within, whereby the right and left channels are inflated like small intestines as they are filled with the slight sound of wind. With respect to **expelling**, imagine that all the winds from the left and right channels flow into the central channel. Without making a sound, swallow some saliva while the upper winds are simultaneously pressed downward upon the navel, whereby you imagine that the winds in the right and left channels are expelled [into the central channel]. After that, the lower winds are gently drawn up from your vajra[57] to the location of the short AH at your navel, and you direct your wind to the short AH and hold it there for as long as you are able. Furthermore, the winds from above and the winds below the navel are drawn together and brought into embrace at your navel. Although in the beginning, you may be able to retain the winds for an extended period of time, because you will not be able to focus your mind on the object of observation for very long, your mind will wander. Therefore, because you will be holding the winds outside of the central channel, you will develop very little heat and bliss, and [your meditation] will be of very little benefit in drawing the winds into the central channel, with the added danger of causing obstacles. You should only restrain the winds until you are about to become uncomfortable.

Regarding **releasing like an arrow**, just before you are no longer able to hold your breath in that way without becoming uncomfortable, you should imagine that [the wind] is gently released and moves upward

56. This refers to the afternoon and morning, respectively.
57. Here, the term "vajra" refers to a penis, but it could just as well be "lotus," which refers to a woman's vagina. Either way, the winds are drawn upward from the lower end of the central channel.

within your central channel very comfortably. You should not imagine that [the wind] exits your body. At this point, you need the two essential points of: (1) imagining that the life-supporting and downward-voiding winds[58] have entered the central channel and been brought into embrace within the central channel at the [navel] channel wheel, and (2) focusing your meditation on the syllable as before. It is certain that when the right and left channels are open, the central channel is closed, and when the central channel is open, the right and left channels are closed; therefore, you are trying to stop the flow of wind through the right and left channels through the vase breathing. Through meditating on these two visualizations for drawing [the winds] into the central channel, you will eventually be able to guide them into the central channel. Furthermore, with the exception of restraining the winds at the navel channel wheel for a short time through your own efforts, they will not naturally abide. Therefore, until that [natural abiding] happens, do not restrain the winds for too long. Instead, you should [gradually] extend the length of time you restrain the winds in accordance with their natural ability to remain.

You should commence with your practice of vase breathing before you have taken your meal or after eating [and digesting] your food, so that your stomach is fully at ease. Don't practice for an extended period of time without breaks. Instead, you should rest and familiarize yourself [with the practices] between sessions.

Next, you should ignite and kindle the inner fire. To ignite the inner fire, you should imagine that the winds below the navel dissolve into the short AH while appropriately practicing meditation on the vase breath, which is similar to stimulating the ignition of a fire in a hearth from which extremely subtle sparks are emitted. By continuing in this way, a very subtle flame erupts from the short AH, crescent moon, drop, and *nada*. The tiny flame becomes increasingly bigger, whereby the channels at the navel channel wheel are illuminated and [the tiny flame] sequentially travels within the central channel, heating up the HUM at your heart, which causes the bodhichitta to drip [from the HUM] and descend

---

58. In the practice of vase breathing, the life-supporting wind is brought down from above and the downward-voiding wind is drawn upward from below.

upon the syllable AH, whereby it [i.e., the flaming AH at your navel] grows even stronger.

The flame strikes the OM at your throat, which is the nature of the fire-wind. It grows bigger and melts the syllable HAM at your crown together with its cushion. It sequentially descends and when it arrives at your throat, you experience joy and you remain there for a short time.

The OM [at your throat] once again melts together with its cushion, and when it arrives at your heart, you generate supreme joy and remain there for a short time.

The HUM at your heart also melts and dissolves into the syllable AM[59] at your navel. You generate extraordinary joy and you remain there for a short time.

The syllable AH blazes even bigger, causing the bodhichitta to descend to your secret place, whereby you generate simultaneously born joy and you meditate single-pointedly.

Focus your attention once again upon the syllable AH at your navel, causing it to blaze even bigger, whereby the light rays of inner fire become radiant, completely illuminating your channels, the interior of your body, your dwelling, your region, and so forth, so that it is as though you can perceive everything directly and [simultaneously] focus your attention upon the short AH.[60] Because of that, you will quickly develop great experiences of clear concentration and realization, and through familiarizing yourself with this you will gain some ability to perceive hidden phenomena; however, it is said that this is not actual clairvoyance.[61]

59. The short AH has a drop upon it that grammatically functions as a diacritical mark, representing the sound "ma" and changing AH to AM.

60. The main object of observation is the short AH, while one small part of the mind is aware of its light rays illuminating your body, environment, and so forth. This is done without letting the mind waver from focusing on the short AH.

61. According to Atisha, you don't attain actual clairvoyance until you have attained tranquil abiding. Thus, although you attain here what many would consider to be clairvoyance, without tranquil abiding it is unstable and somewhat unreliable, so it is not considered to be actual clairvoyance.

How to Cause the Winds to Enter, Abide in, and Dissolve into the Central Channel through Meditating in This Way

With respect to the unmistaken signs of the winds entering, abiding in, and dissolving into the central channel through meditating in this way, once you have ascertained whether the winds are flowing through the right or left nostril at the beginning and end of the session, you continuously focus your wind and mind on the object of observation in accordance with the previous meditation. If, upon examining the nostrils, you find that the winds are moving evenly, that is counted as a definite sign [that the winds have entered the central channel]. As for the term "definite," merely once or twice is not considered a definite sign. If there are no other obstructions [such as blockages in your nostrils], and it occurs each time you focus your attention, that is counted [as a definite sign] and is the meaning of having progressed [to the stage of bringing the winds into the central channel]. If, in addition to moving evenly, they are moving with equal force without either the right or left being weaker or stronger, that is the indication that the winds have merely entered the central channel through the force of that yoga. However, this is not to say that [the winds] won't transfer [back and forth] from the right and left [nostrils after] having entered [the central channel just] one time.[62] This is [the indication that] the winds [are] entering the central channel.

Next, through continuing to meditate intensely as before, the movement of the winds in the two nostrils becomes increasingly weaker. At the conclusion, you should perform a detailed analysis. Finally, the wind becomes so subtle that it stops; this is the indication that it has dissolved. There are two types of dissolution: difficult and easy. For the difficult dissolution, your stomach will feel filled with air for a moment but will then be pacified. As soon as it is pacified, you develop an extraordinary warmth emanating from your navel and secret place. Furthermore, if you quickly generate a very extensive warmth that feels as though it is

---

62. This means that just because you were able to get the winds to enter the central channel, this does not mean that they will stay in the central channel. In fact, they will almost certainly leave the central channel after a short time and transfer back and forth between the right and left channels.

between your muscle and skin, it has not penetrated the correct location. If you generate a small degree of warmth from the center of your body and it is very difficult to generate, you have penetrated the precise point.

Furthermore, if you are predominantly affected by an accumulation of mental sinking because you have not eliminated subtle mental sinking, and if you are not skilled at penetrating the vital point of the navel channel wheel yet repeatedly meditate on vase breathing, [then] you will not be capable of binding the winds within the central channel, and the winds will go to other sites even when the subtle movement of the winds through your two nostrils ceases. The winds may not arise and enter,[63] but you will also not be able to retain them within [the central channel]. Check your abdomen; if it is moving, that is a sign of [the above faults]. If a subtle movement has ceased in your nostrils and if your stomach is also not moving, that is a definite sign [that the winds have entered the central channel].

Regarding the duration of conjoining the winds with the vase breathing, according to the *Samvarodaya Tantra*,[64] place the back of your left hand against the palm of your right hand, rub it three times, and snap your fingers six times. Therefore, rub them once, snap your fingers twice, rub them one more, and snap your fingers twice. Repeat that process once more. This adds up to rubbing the hands three times and snapping your fingers six times. The person with the least capacity can hold the vase breath while doing that thirty-six times; the middling can double that and perform seventy-two; the best can triple [the first number] and perform it one hundred and eight times. This is the duration for carrying out one vase breath when there are no other adverse conditions. If you are able to actually accomplish such a thing, you will also have a long life.

How to Generate the Four Joys in Dependence upon Such Entering has three sections:

1. How to Manifest the Signs and [Cause] the Inner Fire to Blaze
2. How to Generate the Four Joys in Dependence upon Melting the Bodhichitta

---

63. This means there may be no inhalation or exhalation.
64. Tib. *sDom 'byung*.

3. How to Meditate on Simultaneously Born Exalted Wisdom

How to Manifest the Signs and [Cause] the Inner Fire to Blaze

When giving rise to the signs that emerge from causing the winds to enter the central channel, in general the speed with which the winds dissolve into the doors of the senses, the degree of the four signs and the four empties, as well as their duration, rapidity, and so forth—[all these] vary depending upon the degree of the individual's faculties; therefore, there is no definitive standardization. In particular, when accomplishing the single-pointed concentration of tranquil abiding during the perfection vehicle, the generation stage of highest yoga mantra, and so forth, the winds do not enter the central channel, and although some coarse signs may occur, they don't follow a definite sequence, occurring instead in a variety of ways. However, when the winds enter the central channel they do follow a definite sequence.

Regarding the phrase, "For that, initially the earth element dissolves into the water element . . .", as the capacity of your earth element to support your aggregates deteriorates, the water element becomes more apparent and this is conventionally designated as "dissolving." When the earth element dissolves into the water element, you experience the shimmering mirage-like appearance, which is like the hot sun of summer striking a large plain.[65] When the water element dissolves into the fire element, you experience the smoke-like appearance, which is like a fine waft of blue smoke swirling within your dwelling. When the fire element dissolves into the wind element, you experience the fireflies-like appearance, which is like sparks carried by the wind from bundles of grass being burnt in a bonfire during a pitch-black night. As the wind that is the mount of conceptual thought begins to dissolve into consciousness, there is an appearance similar to a burning candle undisturbed by the wind.

Next, as the wind of conceptual thought completely dissolves into the

---

65. This could also be likened to a mirage in a desert, or when you are driving and the summer sun strikes the hot pavement.

mind of appearance, the path of white appearance manifests, which is like a pure autumn sky pervaded by moonlight and is the **first empty**.[66] Next, the [mind of white appearance] dissolves into the mind of increase, whereby the path of red increase manifests, which is like a pure autumn sky pervaded by sunlight and is the **second empty**. [The mind of red increase] dissolves into near-attainment, whereby the mind of black near-attainment manifests, which is like a pure autumn sky pervaded by utter darkness and is the **third empty**. [The mind of black near-attainment] dissolves into the clear light, whereby the clear light manifests, which is like perceiving the natural radiance of the pure autumn sky at dawn that is not polluted or obscured and is free from the three faults of moonlight, sunlight, and darkness. This is the **fourth empty**. Furthermore, although initially the four signs and the four empties will emerge in a variety of sequences, once you have trained sufficiently, they will emerge in a definite sequence.

How to Generate the Four Joys in Dependence upon Melting the Bodhichitta

In dependence upon the special blazing of inner fire within your central channel in that way, the bodhichitta melts and travels through your central channel from your crown to your throat, and you generate joy. It sequentially travels from your throat to your heart, and you generate supreme joy. It sequentially travels from your heart to your navel, and you generate extraordinary joy. It travels from your navel to the tip of your jewel at your secret place, and you generate simultaneously born joy. At the time of the four joys in general and the generation of simultaneously born joy in particular, you should recall the view that all phenomena is without inherent existence and place your mind single-pointedly upon emptiness to the best of your ability. This is how to generate the four joys of descending order. If the bodhichitta is descending through the pathway of the central channel in this way, the wind that would cause its ejaculation is not functioning; therefore, you once again imagine you are drawing the bodhichitta back up your central channel, and when it arrives at

66. The four signs of white appearance, red increase, black near-attainment, and clear light are often referred to as the first, second, third, and fourth empties, respectively. Alternatively, they are referred as empty, very empty, great empty, and all empty, respectively.

the navel, you generate the joy of reverse order. When it arrives at your heart, you experience supreme joy of reverse order. When it arrives at your throat, you experience extraordinary joy of reverse order. When it arrives at your crown, you experience simultaneously born joy of reverse order. This is how to generate the four joys of reverse order.

Furthermore, for each of the four joys of descent and ascent there are divisions of four, such as the "joy of joy" and so forth, making a total of sixteen joys [in each direction]. The four joys of ascent are superior to the four joys of descent. These are comparable to the sixteen phases of the waxing moon and the waning moon. Our text states,

> When the white bodhichitta descends, a small segment of blood [or red bodhichitta] descends along with it. At each of the four places, there are four degrees [of bliss], and each point has its own experience of bliss. Furthermore, you should understand that there is a division of small, middling, and great, based on the descent of the particle of blood [i.e., red bodhichitta] as it reaches each of these four places, creating twelve experiences of bliss.

Although it is possible to ignite the inner fire of the navel and secret place and to experience joy through the descent of the melting bodhichitta to the secret place despite not meditating on the path, [when the inner fire is ignited] in this way, the inner fire will blaze outside of the central channel where the melting of the bodhichitta will occur. Therefore, in general, it is not necessary to dissolve the winds into the central channel to merely melt the bodhichitta.[67] It is for this reason that, through the force of your former meditation, when the bodhichitta melts through the power of dissolving the winds into the central channel and sequentially descends from the crown, because the movement of the wind has shifted to another location,[68] when it arrives at the tip of the jewel, the wind that

67. This means that it is possible to melt the bodhichitta outside of the central channel through various means other than causing the winds to enter, abide in, and dissolve into the central channel. However, these are counterproductive with respect to completion-stage meditations; therefore, we should strive to melt the bodhichitta within the central channel.
68. This means that during ordinary sexual intercourse, the winds are not flowing within the central channel and the ordinary inner fire is igniting in the left channel causing the descent and ejaculation of semen or the release of vaginal secretions. At this point, the winds have

causes the ejaculation of the bodhichitta will not be functioning; therefore, you will be able to retain it at the tip of the jewel without releasing it until you develop a fully qualified simultaneously born [bliss and emptiness]. Because of this, the bodhichitta will not be released, and once you are able to draw it back up [the central channel] and reverse the flow of the bodhichitta, you will not need to [employ the methods to] spread it throughout your body. There are some people who, despite having meditated as previously [described], are unable to dissolve the winds into the central channel yet nevertheless are able to induce bliss through melting the bodhichitta. When inducing the drop in this way, it is extremely difficult to retain it once it reaches the vajra-jewel; therefore, you should reverse it when it is at the upper sites and move it back upward. If you don't spread it out once you have reversed it, you will develop illnesses; therefore, you should disperse it [throughout the channels of your body].[69]

With respect to just how you should induce the diffusion, the melting should proceed slowly in stages without exerting yourself too forcefully, whereby you will be able to gently reverse and disperse [the bodhichitta]. If the melting occurs quickly, you will need to forcefully exert yourself. To do this, you should sit in the vajra posture, tighten the tendons of your four [limbs], contract your fingers and toes, cross your two hands in front of your chest, clench your fists, press the tip of your tongue against your palate, forcefully turn your eyes upward, and suck in your stomach toward your spine. Next, forcefully pull the lower winds upward and verbally recite the long HUM twenty-one times, during which you recite HUM about seven times for each time you draw it upward.[70] Mentally, imagine

---

entered the central channel, which is here termed "another location"; therefore, because the downward-voiding wind that would ordinarily cause ejaculation is no longer functioning, the white bodhichitta can be retained within the central channel.

69. This sometimes happens when practitioners have not properly trained in drawing the winds into the central channel yet persevere in vase breathing. We also see a similar situation in people who seriously pursue kundalini yoga without being properly trained.

70. In his commentary on the five stages of the completion stage of Chakrasamvara of the Ghantapa tradition, the First Panchen Lama, Losang Chökyi Gyaltsen, gives the following description of this process (as translated in Ngulchu Dharmabhadra and Panchen Chökyi Gyaltsen, *The Source of Supreme Bliss: Heruka Chakrasamvara Five Deity Practice and Commentary* [Somerville, MA: Wisdom Publications, 2022], 150–51): "Sit with your legs in the vajra posture. Take the tips of both thumbs and suppress the channel at the [base] of the ring fingers, make a fist and cross them at your heart while pressing down on your two breasts and draw your stomach

that red, hook-like light rays emerge from the syllable HAM at your crown, traveling down the center of your body a little closer to your spine and within your central channel to just below the navel, striking the short AH, whereby it is pulled upward by the wind below until it arrives at the crown.

Having practiced in this way, if your bliss decreases and you develop a very distinct sense of coolness in your stomach, this is a sign of reversal. If you don't disperse it, you will develop illnesses; therefore, you should imagine that it is dispersed from your crown throughout all your channels, like shooting stars or spilt mercury. Gently restrain the lower winds as before and slowly restrain the upper winds and shake your entire body, as done during the practice of the six magical wheels.

How to Meditate on Simultaneously Born Exalted Wisdom

When you have practiced in accordance with the previous explanation for the forward and reverse orders and the bodhichitta arrives at each location, you identify the development of the four joys, and when you recognize the simultaneously born joy in particular—once you have recognized the definite meaning of the view [of emptiness]—[then] remain amid the view while thinking, "I am the inseparability of bliss and emptiness. And what's more, I am the resultant truth body of exalted wisdom." Place your mind in single-pointed meditative equipoise upon the exalted wisdom of nondual bliss and emptiness. [The Mahasiddha] Shridhara [d.u.] states,

> You should remain with your realization of exalted wisdom,
> Whether in every session, once a day,
> [For] half a month, a month, a year,
> An eon, or a thousand eons.

---

in toward your spine. Reverse the eyes upward. As for the visualization, from your crown, light rays radiate in the aspect of two webs that descend through your central channel. At the lower end is a blue letter HUM with its head pointing upward, and these two webs arrive one in front of the other. At the secret place is the single-pronged pink vajra with seed. The two tips hook the shabkyu and the nada, pulling them upward. Then, like a blacksmith who extracts a hot piece of metal with a pair of tongs, imagine that the variegated vajra with seed is drawn upward inside the central channel. With your speech recite the long HUM twenty-one times: three times up the center of the jewel channel wheel, three times to the secret place, three times to the navel, three times to the heart, three times to the throat, and three times to the crown. When you [recite it three more times to make] twenty-one, imagine it dissolves into the channel wheel at the crown. From there imagine the white drop is spread out throughout all the channels."

As this states, you should persevere [with your realization of exalted wisdom]. If you don't have a perfect understanding of the view with bliss alone, you should forsake mental vacillation and place your mind in a state of nonconceptuality. When you arise from that state of meditative equipoise, you should seal with bliss and emptiness all environments and beings, so that all environments and beings that appear in subsequent attainment are empty [of inherent existence]; the emptiness is the deity body, and the deity body appears as great bliss. This is the special means of persevering [with your realization of bliss and emptiness]. Whatever occurs through that method is the meditative stabilization and the yoga of subsequent attainment.

Once again, you should unite the winds and meditate on inner fire, alternating your practice by inducing the four joys of forward and reverse order.

Meditating in Dependence upon a Karma Mudra as the Outer Condition

Once you actualize realizations through meditating in that way and are about to attain the ultimate example clear light of isolated mind, you must rely upon a karma mudra, since you will not be able to induce that [realization] through the inner condition of meditating on yoga alone.[71] In that way, if we divide the types of karma mudras according to their types [of occupation, we have] (1) the butcher, (2) the dancer, (3) the flower-garland maker, and (4) the dyer. If we divide them according to the shapes of the lower ends of their central channel, we have (1) the lotus, (2) the conch, (3) the deer, and (4) the elephant—with the lotus type as the best. If we divide them according to their realizations, there are three types of dakinis: (1) mantra born, (2) field born, and (3) spontaneously born.

A mantra-born dakini is a woman who has trained her mental continuum in the common path and subsequently obtained the complete empowerment of highest yoga tantra. She perfectly protects her commitments and vows. With such a foundation, she is skilled in the meditations

71. If we are to bring *all* the winds, including the subtle pervasive wind in its entirety, into the indestructible drop at the heart prior to death, we must rely upon a qualified karma mudra.

of the generation stage, and through her extensive meditation has begun to generate the realizations of the lower levels of the completion stage. A field-born dakini is someone born in the twenty-four holy places and so forth. A spontaneously born dakini is someone with some degree of the clear light of union.

Furthermore, both objects of support[72] must be fully qualified to practice this path. For this, they must have perfected their training in the entering, abiding, and dissolving of the winds within the central channel, causing the bodhichitta to descend to the tip of the jewel while being able to retain it without ejaculation, and so forth.

There are those who have not developed even a rough approximation of [such qualifications] yet who practice in dependence upon quotes from some false oral tradition, pretending that what they are doing is profound when in fact it is utterly inappropriate. The *Heruka Tantra Samvarodaya*[73] states,

> When the Dharma of yoga without yoga
> Becomes intercourse with a mudra,
> It is the way of wisdom without wisdom;
> Have no doubt that you will be going to hell.

As I explained earlier, by meditating properly on the stages of the path, you will be able to retain the bodhichitta at the tip of the jewel without it seeping out and so forth. The authentic texts of the mahasiddhas state that if you develop fully qualified experiences and realizations, you should rely upon a karma mudra as the cooperative condition for generating the four joys. Therefore, [after having developed these qualifications,] you should cultivate the four joys by relying upon a karma mudra as the cooperative condition for developing the four joys. Therefore, initially you should learn from other sources the way to practice in dependence upon the profound inner and outer methods, such as a mantra-born dakini who is skilled in the sixty-four arts of love and so forth. Those who are unable to rely upon a karma mudra in this way should meditate for a long time

---

72. This is referring to both the male and the female practitioner who will be practicing the yoga of union.
73. Tib. *rGyud he ru ka mngon 'byung.*

on a wisdom mudra [in the aspect of] Vajrayogini and so forth. If they attain stable clear appearance and divine pride through [meditating on a wisdom mudra], when they develop simultaneously born joy through abiding in this absorption, they should meditate on the union of bliss and emptiness. Alternatively, if you are unable to, you should develop simultaneously born bliss and place your mind in single-pointed concentration upon that [bliss].

How to Meditate on the Illusory Body and the Clear Light in Dependence upon That has two sections:

1. A GENERAL PRESENTATION OF HOW TO MEDITATE ON THE REMAINING PATHS IN DEPENDENCE UPON INNER FIRE
2. HOW TO MEDITATE ON THE INDIVIDUAL PATHS

A General Presentation of How to Meditate on the Remaining Paths in Dependence upon Inner Fire

How to meditate on the illusory body and clear light in dependence upon drawing the winds into the central channel through meditating on the inner fire of this system is clarified by relying upon the Guhyasamaja [teachings], and [in particular upon] the lineage of the Arya tradition of Guhyasamaja coming from Marpa. Furthermore, until the winds enter, abide in, and dissolve into the central channel, you will not be able to generate the concentrations of appearance, increase, and attainment through inducing the isolated mind of example clear light. Regarding the attainment of the completely qualified clear light of the example clear light of isolated mind, which realizes emptiness through a generic image with simultaneously born bliss,[74] in the very first moment that your winds stir from that clear light, you accomplish the black near-attainment of reverse order within the heart of your old aggregates, and in the second moment

---

74. The "ultimate example clear light of isolated mind" is accomplished when all the winds are caused to enter, abide in, and dissolve into the indestructible drop within the central channel at the heart. At this point, the mind of clear light will be fully actualized, and it is only the realization of emptiness that needs to be improved. Because all the winds have been drawn into the indestructible drop, you now have access to the most subtle wind associated with the most subtle mind of clear light. Because of this, when you begin to arise from the clear light, the subtle winds will arise in the form of the deity.

you arise in the actual impure illusory body as the stage of "self-blessing"[75] separately from your old aggregates. The mind of black near-attainment of reverse order is the first mind of that illusory body; therefore, the place where you initially accomplish the illusory body is in the heart of your old aggregates.

Next, when that illusory body once again enters your old aggregates, you engage in the activities of subsequent attainment. In that way, that yogi [or yogini] familiarizes himself with his experience and realization for a short time, after which he will perceive signs that he is about to attain the meaning clear light. At dawn he relies upon the skillful means of the outer and inner conditions, and the example clear light accomplished from mere wind and mind is purified within the meaning clear light, whereby he will receive signs of the winds entering, abiding in, and dissolving into the central channel and will unite the four joys and the four empties. During that simultaneously born clear light, the mind is placed single-pointedly upon bliss and emptiness, whereby that [impure] illusory body disappears like a cloud in the sky. Simultaneously with the cessation of the black near-attainment of reverse order that emerges from the meaning clear light, that meaning clear light undoubtedly abandons the delusion-obstructions [to liberation], whereby you accomplish [both] the uninterrupted path and the meaning clear light that directly realizes emptiness with a mind of simultaneously born bliss.[76]

When you begin to arise from that meditative stabilization, that meaning clear light functions as the cooperative condition, and the uncon-

---

75. "Self-blessing" is the name for the third stage in the structure of the five stages of the completion stage as set forth in the Guhyasamaja teachings, and is synonymous with the illusory body.
76. This is one of the most distinctive features of highest yoga tantra. In the sutra tradition of the perfection vehicle, when a person newly attains a direct realization of emptiness he or she moves to the first bodhisattva ground and abandons the intellectually formed afflictive emotions. It is not until one countless eon later, upon the attainment of the eighth bodhisattva ground, that such a practitioner abandons the delusion-obstructions that prevent liberation. Here in highest yoga tantra, the practitioner is able to newly attain a direct realization of emptiness, and abandon both intellectually formed afflictive emotions and the innate obstructions to liberation simultaneously, thereby accomplishing in one session what would take one countless eon to accomplish through the perfection vehicle. Additionally, he or she attains a special pure illusory body that is capable of sending forth countless emanation bodies and that will directly transform into the enjoyment body upon enlightenment, which is something not even spoken of in the perfection vehicle.

taminated wind of five-colored light that is the mount of that clear light functions as the substantial cause through which you arise in the pure illusory body in a location separate from your old aggregates—[namely,] in the pure illusory body adorned with the marks and signs that is the actual body of a learner's union.[77] At the same time, the signs of reverse order, beginning with the [mind of black] near-attainment up to the mirage-like appearance, manifest.

Furthermore, when that meaning clear light ceases, you accomplish the mind of black near-attainment of reverse order, abandon delusion-obstructions, and attain the path of liberation—and the person [who has done this] has become an arhat. At the same time, you attain the union of abandonment. With such a union, you don't need to rely upon a karma mudra for your spiritual practice, and by merely placing your mind in single-pointed meditative equipoise upon emptiness, your winds will enter, abide in, and dissolve into your central channel, and the signs and empties will arise exactly in accordance [with death].[78] Once you conjoin bliss and emptiness during that simultaneously born clear light, your body of the pure illusory body and your pure mind of ultimate truth become one taste in the meaning clear light, and you attain union that is the realization of body and mind becoming one in actuality. When you arise from that clear light, you arise in a body that is separate from your old aggregates and adorned with the signs and indications, [and] that has a multitude of coarse and subtle emanation bodies. If you wish to arise from that meditative stabilization, you enter the heart of your old aggregates and engage in the activities of subsequent attainment. Thus, during that meditative equipoise, it is the union of realization.[79] During subsequent attainment, you must

77. This is a reference to the union of the meaning clear light and the pure illusory body, which is a "learner's union" in that it still has further to go on the path to enlightenment, whereas the union of no-more-learning is synonymous with enlightenment.

78. One of the goals of the completion stage is to cause all the winds to enter the central channel exactly at the time of death. In this way, you are able to utilize the full potential of your clear light mind to realize emptiness.

79. The union of abandonment occurs when you newly attain meaning clear light and then you arise in the pure illusory body. The union of realization occurs during the next session, when you once again enter into meditative equipoise on the meaning clear light.

arise from the mind of meaning clear light; therefore this is the union of abandonment.

Furthermore, [there is a system for] apprehending the clear light of sleep through the force of wind during sleep in dependence upon the winds entering the central channel during waking.[80] [And there is another system] where you utilize a reliable factor of stable concentration common to the Hinayana and Mahayana during waking and place your mind in a state of concentration prior to going to sleep, and [then] combine it with sleep or, alternatively, concentrate on a mere portion of emptiness; therefore, it is a grave error to mistake this [second system] for the clear light of sleep that comes from causing the winds to enter the central channel.

You must not mistake the special techniques for apprehending dreams through the force of wind with apprehending them through the force of aspiration. When apprehending them through the force of wind, there are unique methods employed that blend the clear light of sleep and arising in the enjoyment body in the intermediate state.[81] If the winds enter, abide in, and dissolve into the central channel while you are awake, you will be able to apprehend the clear light of sleep and dreams through the force of wind. If that occurs, your yoga of waking will be greatly enhanced, and your practice during sleep will be greatly assisted by your practices while awake.

[The Nine Mixings]

There are three mixings during waking, three mixings during sleep, and three mixings during death, which [together] are referred to as "the instructions of the nine mixings" and are widely renowned as profound instructions.

80. This means that through the force of your accomplishment in causing the winds to enter, abide in, and dissolve into the central channel through meditation during waking, you are able to induce the mind of clear light at the time of sleep and meditate on emptiness, which should in no way be confused with other systems in which you merely recall emptiness while falling asleep and attempt to carry that understanding through the sleep process.

81. For more details on this aspect of the Six Yogas, see Tsongkhapa Lobzang Drakpa, *Tsongkhapa's Six Yogas of Naropa*, trans. and ed. Glenn H. Mullin (Ithaca, NY: Snow Lion Publications, 1996).

Vajrayogini

[1.] Mixing the Truth Body during Waking: Furthermore, if the winds enter your central channel and you then bring your practice of the inner fire and vase breathing up to your heart while relying upon the outer and inner methods,[82] [then] your winds will enter, abide in, and dissolve [into the heart channel wheel], and the four joys will emerge as the nature of the four empties.[83] During the simultaneously born joy of the clear light, you should place your mind in single-pointed meditative equipoise as the actual truth-body mind of the Conqueror.

[2.] Mixing the Enjoyment Body during Waking: When you arise from that clear light, you accomplish the three minds of [black] near-attainment, [red] increase, and [white] appearance, together with their four signs in reverse order. You arise as Vajrayogini with a white-colored body tinged red, separately from your old aggregates.[84] Train in establishing divine pride that that body is the actual resultant enjoyment body.

[3.] Mixing the Emanation Body during Waking: When you once again arise from that meditative stabilization, you unobstructedly enter into the heart of your old aggregates and assume the coarse emanation body.

[4.] Mixing the Truth Body during Sleep: When such a yogi [or yogini] is about to go to sleep, he emanates light rays from the HUM at his heart, which collect all worlds and their beings into himself. He is also absorbed from below and above, up to the nada of the HUM. Once you imagine that that nada is also absorbed into the clear light, you fall asleep, whereby the winds enter, abide in, and dissolve into your central channel, together

---

82. The outer method is relying upon a karma mudra, and the inner method is the yoga of the channels, winds, and drops.

83. This means that as you experience the four joys, you will simultaneously experience the four empties. For example, as the bodhichitta descends from your crown to your throat, you will experience joy and the mind of white appearance. When it reaches your heart, you will experience the mind of red increase and supreme joy. When it reaches your navel, you will experience the mind of black near-attainment and extraordinary joy. And when it reaches the lower tip of your central channel, you will experience the mind of clear light and simultaneously born joy.

84. At this point, your Vajrayogini body is white because it is established from the life-supporting wind, which is white in color.

with the corresponding signs. During the simultaneously born clear light, the bodhichitta is collected at the heart, and with that bliss you combine bliss and emptiness and place your mind in single-pointed equipoise.

[5.] Mixing the Enjoyment Body during Sleep: Next, when the dream state is about to commence, contemplate, "I must arise in the complete enjoyment body," and with that intention meditate on the dream body as the body of Vajrayogini.

[6.] Mixing the Emanation Body during Sleep: When you are about to awaken from sleep, you enter the heart of your old aggregates without obstruction, whereby the winds begin flowing through your nostrils, objective appearances arise, whatever appears is empty, that emptiness is bliss, and that [manifestation] of bliss is regarded as the deity body. You should sequentially train in these three objects of knowledge.

Thus, if you are able to arise in the special illusory body of dreams at the conclusion of apprehending the clear light of sleep, through familiarizing yourself with that, your capacity to practice during waking will be empowered. Through that, you will also achieve great power in your yoga during sleep. In this life, such a yogi has attained a most excellent state, and when he practices at death, through the force of his familiarity with the clear light of sleep and the illusory body of dreams, and their similarity with apprehending the clear light of death and the illusory body of the intermediate state, no other [impure] appearances will arise. These are two of the most amazing and highly praised incontrovertible oral instructions.[85]

How to Meditate on the Individual Paths has two sections:

1. HOW TO MEDITATE ON THE ILLUSORY BODY
2. HOW TO MEDITATE ON THE CLEAR LIGHT

---

85. More detail on the nine mixings can be found in the second text in this book. Or, for an even more detailed and absolutely stunning presentation of the nine mixings, see Pabongkha Dechen Nyingpo, *The Secret Revelations of Chittamani Tara: A Profound Commentary on the Two Stages* (Somerville, MA: Wisdom Publications, 2023).

How to Meditate on the Illusory Body has three sections:

1. How to Meditate on Appearances as Illusory
2. How to Meditate on Dreams as Illusory
3. How to Meditate on the Intermediate State as Illusory

How to Meditate on Appearances as Illusory

The person with the best faculties has the capacity to perfectly collect the winds into the central channel, whereby he will meditate on mixing during waking and during sleep, which is something I don't need to explain [again] at this point. Although the person of middling capacity has not previously [caused the winds] to enter, abide in, and dissolve, he has reached a definitive understanding of the view of emptiness and has perfected the generation stage and so forth, conjoined inseparably with simultaneously born great bliss. He places his mind in single-pointed meditative stabilization, and when arising from that mental stabilization, he perceives things within the state of subsequent attainment, whereby whatever appears is perceived as an illusory supporting and supported mandala. At this point, these arise naturally and don't need to be practiced separately.

If you are not capable of that, you are a person of lesser faculties, so you familiarize yourself with the mere bliss in meditative equipoise. When you arise from that meditative stabilization, you regard whatever ordinary appearances of the world and its beings you see with your eyes in subsequent attainment—such as persons, animals, mountains, and so forth, or whatever appears to your mind—as mere conceptual imputations that are established upon their individual basis of imputation, without even one atom existing inherently from its own side, and you come to a definitive conclusion concerning this through logical reasoning, such as "the absence of being one or many" and so forth.[86] Previously,

---

86. This line of reasoning investigates whether an inherently existing object is inherently one with its object or inherently separate from it. This reasoning is included with the sevenfold analysis as well as the fourfold analysis. The latter utilizes four steps: (1) identifying the object of negation, (2) realizing that whatever is neither inherently one nor inherently many does not inherently exist, (3) establishing that it is not inherently one, and (4) establishing that it is not inherently many. This results in the understanding that the object of analysis does not inherently exist.

while neither examining nor analyzing, things were falsely appearing as though inherently established, yet if it seems that nothing exists and those appearances become mere nothingness—causing you to wonder "Does nothing exist at all?"—[then] you should induce absolute certainty that they exist as mere conventional designations that are merely imputed by names and concepts, and that, logically, action and agent, cause and effect are all nondeceptive, yet whatever appears is [nevertheless also] not truly existent, like an illusion. Furthermore, all these [appearances] have become the nature of your mind of simultaneously born bliss, and with that [mind] you ascertain emptiness that is the absence of inherent existence of all phenomena, and [realize that] the apprehended objects of that bliss and emptiness are gods, goddesses, celestial mansions, and so forth.

In this way, train your mind to perceive everything as nothing but limitless purity arising as the illusory-like deity body. You once again enter into meditative stabilization whereby, if you have accomplished simultaneously born great bliss, from that perspective you recollect the view of emptiness and place your mind single-pointedly upon that bliss and emptiness. You should continue in this way, alternating between meditative stabilization and subsequent attainment.

How to Meditate on Dreams as Illusory has four sections:

1. Apprehending Dreams
2. Purifying and Increasing
3. Abandoning Fear and Training in the Illusory
4. Meditating on the Suchness of Dreams

Apprehending Dreams

[You will be able] to apprehend dreams through the force of wind once you are able to cause the winds to enter, abide in, and dissolve into the central channel while awake. While sleeping, you will be able to apprehend both the clear light of sleep and [also] dreams through the force of wind; therefore, these topics have already been covered [in the previous explanation]. Here, I shall explain how to apprehend [dreams] through the force of determination, by continuously recalling your resolution throughout the day. Regarding this method, you should repeatedly train in your determination by contemplating, "Everything that appears throughout the day is a dream. I must recognize dreams as dreams and continue with my spiritual practices during my dreams." Regarding the appearance of dreams at night, train in a very strong determination by thinking, "Come what may, I must recognize dreams." For a few gifted individuals, this is all that will be required to recognize their dreams. To apprehend dreams, you should have a clear mind and sleep lightly. You will not be able to apprehend dreams if you have a dull mind and sleep heavily.

Regarding the way to recognize [dreams] through forceful means at night, you should avoid busyness, as a means of gaining clarity; not wear extremely heavy clothes; not eat greasy food; and make a clear distinction between foods that are impure and those that are pure.

Meditate on guru yoga as you are about to go to sleep, or, alternatively, focus on the guru as the lord of the lineage [on your crown as the deity] and as the embodiment of all personal deities. You should make extremely powerful, heartfelt supplications to him, such as "As I sleep, may my coarse wind and mind be free from all activity." Offer a torma to the dakinis and Dharma protectors and entrust them with the enlightened actions of assisting you in apprehending dreams and so forth.

Regarding the actual way to employ forceful methods of recognition, when lying down, visualize yourself as the deity and, if you are capable, visualize the three channels and the six channel wheels in the center of your body. If that is beyond your capacity, visualize the channel wheel at your throat and, in the center of that, visualize a moon seat with a red syllable OM the size of a mustard seed within the central channel. Imagine that red light rays radiate from the syllable OM and white light rays radiate from the moon seat, both in the aspect of glistening light; think, "I must recognize dreams as soon as they occur," and go to sleep with this very powerful determination.

If you don't recognize [your dreams utilizing that method], continue trying. If, despite your best efforts, you still can't recognize [your dreams], since sleep is the lightest between dawn and when the sun rises over the eastern mountains, you should make supplications at that time, combined with the same determination as before.[87] Visualize a white drop the size

---

87. This means that you awaken just before dawn, perform the following exercises, and go back

of a mustard seed within the central channel at the point between the eyebrows of yourself visualized as the deity and focus your mind upon it. Draw your winds upward with the vase breath and imagine that they dissolve into the drop between your eyebrows; perform this seven times, focus your mind [on the drop], and go back to sleep. If you cannot get to sleep or are quickly awakened from sleep, you should focus your mind upon a black drop the size of a mustard seed upon a moon seat within the lower end of your central channel after pressing down the upper wind [by utilizing the vase breath] seven times. To lighten your sleep, focus your attention on the radiant [drop] at the upper end [of your central channel,] between your eyebrows. To sleep more soundly, meditate on a dark drop at the lower end of your central channel at your secret place. In this way, you should pay special attention to creating a balance between the two. If you are unable to apprehend [your dreams] because your sleep is too heavy at dusk and your sleep is too light at dawn, you should find the appropriate balance of dusk and dawn.

If you are unable to apprehend [your dreams] despite having employed the previous methods for months or even years, it is because you are unable to cause the winds to enter, abide in, and dissolve into the central channel through meditating on inner fire; therefore, once you induce certainty that inner fire is the cornerstone of the path, you should sincerely apply yourself to bringing the winds into the central channel. This is like the quote from Je [Tsongkhapa] Rinpoche's teaching [on the Six Yogas] that states, "Abandoning the root in pursuit of the branches."[88]

Purifying and Increasing

With respect to purifying and increasing dreams, for "purifying"[89] you are purifying faults and training in good qualities. Purifying faults is something like washing impurities. Training in good qualities would be something akin to training in good qualities such as writing and math-

---

to sleep.

88. See Tsongkhapa, *Tsongkhapa's Six Yogas of Naropa*, p. 181.

89. The term being translated here is *sbyang* in Tibetan, which has numerous meanings, such as "cleanse," "purify," "practice," "train," "overcome," "conquer," and "accomplish." Here, Ngulchu Dharmabhadra is using the same term to refer to purifying faults and training in good qualities.

ematics. With respect to "increasing," this refers to increasing and multiplying [objects in your dreams] from one to two, from two to four, and so on, up to one hundred or one thousand, as well as retracting the multitude into a singularity and so forth. In this way, you should train in emanating and retracting.

There are two ways of liberating the illusory nature of dreams: the mundane and the supramundane. With respect to training in liberating the mundane, once you realize you are dreaming, employ introspection by thinking, "This a dream," and within that state, emanate something new that did not previously exist [in your dream], and also transform whatever previously existed, such as fire, water, and so forth. Practice riding the rays of the sun and traveling to the heavenly realms, such as the Realm of the Thirty-Three on the peak of Mount Meru. Having traveled there, have a look around, meditate on your body in whatever way seems appropriate, fly around your abode and go to other realms to see what's there, transform appearances and conceptions by purifying ordinary appearances and conceptions, and so forth. In this way you should train yourself with a variety of exercises.

With respect to training in liberating the supramundane, you should travel to various pure lands, such as Sukhavati, Abhirati, Akanishta, Kechara, Tushita, Copper-Colored Mountain, and so forth. Once there, you should meet with buddhas and bodhisattvas, present offerings, listen to the Dharma, and so forth. The bodhisattva Chagdor Norbu had a dream in which he stole Milarepa's relics from the funeral pyre, after which a dakini emerged and stole them back. Again, a female pig came, and he, emanating himself as a male pig, entered into sexual embrace, and he traveled through numerous worldly realms to try to meet Milarepa in the Abhirati Pure Land in the eastern direction. Having awoken from the dream, he regretted not being able to meet Milarepa. In this way, we should train in appearances through a variety of avenues.

Abandoning Fear and Training in the Illusory

Regarding the abandonment [of fear], once you abandon fear of whatever appears in your dreams, such as fire, water, and so forth, you should directly subjugate them. And when a great wave arises, you should think, "How could this possibly carry me away?" and by transcending it [in this way], you should dive into it and so forth. When a great fire bursts forth, you should think, "This fire is a dream, how could it possibly burn me? My body is a dream body, how could it burn me?" and jump into [the fire] and so forth.

To train in the illusory is very important; therefore, you should induce a consciousness ascertaining the lack of true existence by thinking that whatever appears in your dreams is not truly existent and is similar to illusions that appear yet are nonexistent. Once you have that understanding, you should train in purifying all worlds and beings in your dreams, and in manifesting them in the aspect of the supporting and supported mandala. Furthermore, you should train in manifesting inseparable bliss and emptiness as the mandala in accordance with your practice while awake.

Meditating on the Suchness of Dreams

This is the principal practice; therefore, when dreams arise, you should meditate on yourself appearing clearly in the body of Venerable Vajrayogini. Light rays radiate from the syllable HUM upon a moon seat at your heart, transforming all dream worlds and [dream] beings into light, which is retracted and dissolves into you. You also dissolve in stages up to the nada of the HUM at your heart. The nada is also purified into unobservable emptiness, which you apprehend without wavering. Furthermore, it is much easier to withdraw appearances to the mind during a dream than [to withdraw] appearances to the mind while awake. Because most of the extremely coarse winds dissolve into your heart during sleep, the winds will once again be collected into your heart with great force; therefore, dreams will not arise and you will fall asleep. At that point, you should ascertain the empties;[90] alternatively, if you are unable to ascertain them from the outset, through familiarizing yourself with this practice you will eventually be able to.

Once you gain a little stability in the stages of withdrawal and the empties, it will greatly enhance your meditation of conjoining the winds [with the vase breath] and so forth during waking, and your practice while awake will in turn enhance your practice during sleep.

90. This refers to the four empties mentioned earlier—white appearance, red increase, black near-attainment, and the clear light—which are known as empty, very empty, great empty, and all empty, respectively.

How to Meditate on the Intermediate State as Illusory has two sections:

1. PRESENTING THE GENERAL THESIS OF THE INTERMEDIATE STATE
2. PRESENTING THE STAGES OF PRACTICE

Presenting the General Thesis of the Intermediate State

A brief presentation of the intermediate state is set forth in [Asanga's] summary:[91]

> Name, body, shape, color,
> Full size, manner of moving, manner of seeing,
> Food, karma, and power,
> Sign, lifespan, and manner of rebirth.

In this way, there are thirteen unique attributes:

1. *Unique name*: It is called "the intermediate state of becoming," "arisen from the mind," and "searching for existence."

2. *Unique body*: It is accomplished from the mere wind and mind and has complete sense faculties.

3. *[Unique] shape*: There are numerous opinions about the meaning of the phrase "possessing the shape of its former existence."[92] According to the assertion of Je [Tsongkhapa] Rinpoche, it means the bodily shape of one's place of rebirth in the next life.[93]

---

91. Tib. *bsDus pa'i sdom*.

92. This is a quote from Vasubandhu's *Treasury of Abhidharma* (Abhidharmakośa, Tib. *Chos mngon pa'i mdzod*), ch. 3, v. 13.

93. This is addressed in detail in Pabongkha Dechen Nyingpo, *The Extremely Secret Dakini of Naropa*, p. 118, which states, "The Abhidharmakosha says, 'He will have the form of his previous existence,' and some people can't understand the intended meaning and think that 'previous existence' means that in the intermediate state he will take the form of his predecessor and assert that he has that body. Still others who read the texts say that he will have the shape of the body of his next life. They assert that for the length of seven days, half are in [the form] of the previous life and half are [in the form] of the forthcoming life, as is explained in *The Tibetan Book of the Dead*. According to the *Great Exposition on the Stages of the Path*, this is senseless babbling

4. *[Unique] color*: In general, for those who have engaged in virtue, the appearance of the intermediate state is a white pathway, like moonbeams; for those who have engaged in nonvirtue, the appearance is pitch black or like a black curtain. In particular, for someone who is going to take rebirth in hell, the intermediate state is like a burning log; for those [destined to be born] as animals, it is like smoke; for those [destined to be born] as hungry ghosts, it is like water; for those [destined to be born] as a god or human, it is like gold; and for those [destined to be born] in the form realm, it is like moonlight. If someone is going to be born in the formless realm, he [or she] produces the aggregates of a formless being in the place where he died, so he doesn't have an intermediate state, yet he will have an intermediate state if he is next going to take rebirth downward, in the form realm.

5. *[Unique] full size*: From the perspective of the desire realm, it [i.e., the intermediate-state being] is about the size of a young [human] body between the ages of five and ten.

6. *[Unique] manner of moving*: The intermediate-state [being] of someone

---

that comes from not understanding the intended meaning of the great scriptures. The word 'previous' in 'previous existence' has the translation equivalent [in Sanskrit] of 'purwa' and can mean either 'before' [as in ahead of] or 'predecessor.' If the intermediate state beings reverted to their previous life, then [this interpretation] would be acceptable, but this is not how it is. They are transmigrators moving from a previous life to a later one; therefore it must be that it is 'ahead' of their previous life and the next life is 'ahead' of the intermediate state. Therefore the intermediate state beings must have the form of their future life.

"Not only that, but other than those of a similar type (that is, those with intermediate-state bodies) or those with the 'divine eye,' no one can see an intermediate-state being. According to the previous explanation concerning their lifespan, after seven days, they migrate to another rebirth. Other than that, it is impossible for them to remain any longer. Also, there are demons, hungry ghosts, and so forth who deceive worldly beings and close relatives, [pretending they are] those [loved ones] who have already moved on from the intermediate state.

"Previously, when the Shakya Gache died, the non-Buddhists were performing the funeral services and summoned his spirit, at which point Gache appeared. The Buddhist Upasikas were very surprised and asked the Bhagavan about this. The Bhagavan said, 'This is not anything amazing as he didn't really appear.' 'Well then, who did?' they asked. 'It was some kind of yaksha such as Tokdo or the gandharva Kyabche who transformed into the [aspect of the deceased] and subsequently appeared,' was his reply. The Bonpos have rituals for the deceased where they summon their body and perform cleansing rituals that Jetsun Milarepa talks about in his *Hundred Thousand Songs*."

who is going to hell will travel upside down on his [or her] head, hungry ghosts and animals will travel straight ahead, and the intermediate state [being] of someone going to a happy rebirth will travel upward.

7. *[Unique] manner of seeing*: They can see others of a similar type—for instance, human beings in the intermediate state can see each other—and one of their types of clairvoyance is the divine eye, yet others cannot see them.

8. *Unique food*: They eat only scents.

9. *Unique karma*: Living beings in the intermediate state are propelled by the force of the good and bad karma they have accumulated, and although they may have accomplished an intermediate state of a happy rebirth, if they accumulate nonvirtuous karma, their place of rebirth will change into a bad rebirth. Conversely, although they have accomplished an intermediate state of a lower rebirth, if their friends and relatives who are still alive cultivate virtue on their behalf, [the intermediate state] can transform into to a place of happy rebirth.

10. *[Unique] power and strength*: With the exception of their place of rebirth, they are able to travel anywhere and arrive there by merely thinking of it.

11. *[Unique] sign*: The sun and moon do not appear [to them], and their bodies cast no shadows, they don't leave footprints, and no matter how much they try to speak with their relatives, they are unable to respond.[94] As [another] definite sign, there are terrifying sounds emerging from the elements, such as crashing earth, water, fire, and wind. As an indefinite sign, a variety of joys and sorrows appear [in relation to] their abodes and companions.[95]

---

94. There are five definite signs in the intermediate state: (1) they don't leave footprints, cast a shadow, or make sounds from their bodies; (2) they can move unimpeded through matter; (3) they have clairvoyance; (4) their voices cannot be heard by their relatives; and (5) they don't see the sun or moon.

95. There are six uncertain signs: (1) dwelling place, (2) companions, (3) food and clothing, (4) support, (5) behavior, and (6) mental occurrences.

12. *[Unique] lifespan*: The length of their life is seven days, and if they don't find the conditions for rebirth, they continue in this way for forty-nine days, transferring their existence [from one intermediate-state body to the next] in a series of seven days.

13. *[Unique] manner of taking rebirth*: From among the four places of rebirth, (i) for a miraculous birth, there is attraction to that place; (ii) for a rebirth through heat and moisture, [they are attracted to] the scent; and (iii & iv) for an egg birth and for a womb birth, they see their parents having intercourse as though it were a dream, and take rebirth through strong attachment and anger.

Although at this point in the table of contents of Je [Tsongkhapa's] text entitled *Concise Notes on the Five Stages*[96] there isn't a summation [of blending the three types of intermediate state], there are notes that were actually composed by Je Naropa entitled *A Clear Summary of the Five Stages*,[97] which are in vajra words [and] in which he speaks of "blending the three types of intermediate state." These three are (1) the intermediate state between birth and death, which is the period between being born and dying; (2) the intermediate state of becoming, between dying and the point when you find a place of rebirth; and (3) the intermediate state of dreams, while asleep. With respect to blending the three intermediate states, this refers to the instruction on the nine rounds of mixing.

An ordinary being will experience these as his [or her] forthcoming birth, death, and intermediate state. For a yogi, initially they are the three bodies of the path, and ultimately they arise as the three resultant bodies and have a unique similarity and relationship with the three factors of the basis, path, and result; therefore, they are presented so that the name of the result is given to the cause and the result is named after the cause.[98]

96. Tib. *Rim lnga bsdus pa'i zin bris.*
97. Tib. *Rim lnga bsdus pa gsal ba.*
98. Je Tsongkhapa addresses this point in his commentary *Endowed with the Three Inspirations*, p. 43a, where he states, "An ordinary being will experience these as his [or her] forthcoming birth, death, and intermediate state. For a yogi endowed with the oral instructions, initially they are the three bodies of the path that ultimately arise as the three resultant bodies. In dependence upon their special similarity and relationship, the three basic phenomena are nominally imputed onto the three bodies of the path and result, and the three bodies are nominally imputed onto the three basic phenomena [of birth, death, and the intermediate state]. I have

Presenting the Stages of Practice

For the person who is going to seize [the opportunity presented in] the intermediate state, there are those beings of best, middling, and inferior faculties. Regarding the best, this is someone who in this life has perfected the yoga of the generation stage, and once he [or she] sequentially generates the exalted wisdom of the four joys and the four empties in dependence upon causing the winds to enter, abide in, and dissolve into the central channel through the second stage, he is very close to accomplishing the actual illusory body. However, if he doesn't acquire all the components for engaging in the [tantric] activities in this life, he will not be able to accomplish the illusory body in this life.

Furthermore, with respect to the basis for accomplishing the illusory body, all the coarse and subtle karmic winds dissolve into your heart in exact accordance with the stages of death, whereby the example clear light of isolated mind arises. When emerging from the clear light, the wind that is its mount functions as the substantial cause through which you attain the illusory body. Next, although the yogi [or yogini] is capable of collecting all the coarse karmic winds into the indestructible drop within the central channel at his heart through the force of meditation, he is not able to collect the very subtle pervasive wind; therefore, he must rely upon a karma mudra as the outer condition. If he is not able to find a fully qualified karma mudra, he will not be able to attain the illusory body in this life. Instead, at the time of death all the coarse and subtle winds will naturally dissolve into the heart, and by conjoining that with the practice of yoga, he will actualize example clear light. When he arises from that, he will accomplish the enjoyment body of the path, accomplished from his mere wind and mind as a substitute for the basic constituent of [what would have been] his forthcoming intermediate state.

For a person of middling [faculties], the four empties are generated

---

already extensively explained this elsewhere, together with its sources. Therefore, for now I will merely state that while awake, the illusory body is created in a way that is similar to the intermediate state; therefore, this is also sometimes nominally imputed as 'the intermediate state.' Likewise, when we enter the clear light of sleep, the illusory body of dreams is produced in a way similar to the intermediate state, and therefore is also nominally imputed as 'the intermediate state of dreams.' For a special person [of high realizations], at the conclusion of the clear light of death, he generates the enjoyment body in lieu of an intermediate state body; therefore, this is also called 'the intermediate state.'"

from the wind dissolving into the central channel that is to be purified. If, in addition to that, he is also able to blend emptiness during sleep, that is excellent. For [the person of] the least [faculties], although he is unable to cause the winds to enter, abide in, and dissolve into the central channel in this life, once he has received the empowerments in their entirety and properly protected his commitments and vows, he should properly apply himself to the generation stage. By learning the procedures for meditation on the completion stage, he will establish imprints [for such practices in the future].

As death is approaching these [last] two types, they prepare by forsaking their attachments through giving away all their possessions to virtuous ends, and either receive an empowerment from their guru or properly take self-initiation on their own, whereby they restore whatever defiled vows they may have. For the sake of recalling the instructions on death and the intermediate state, the middling person should meditate on his spiritual practices.

The lesser person also trains repeatedly in familiarizing himself with the means of collecting the winds into the central channel, inducing the four empties, and the system for arising in the deity body, as well as the special systems for training in emptiness during sleep and arising in the illusory body during dreams.

Both [persons of middling and persons of lesser faculties] meditate on the guru-deity in the space before them, make offerings and praises, and make numerous powerful supplications to be able to mix the clear light of death, to be able to mix the intermediate state with the illusory body, and so forth.

Next, regarding the signs of death in brief, there are the four signs, such as the mirage-like appearance due to the earth element dissolving into the water element and so forth, as well as the four empties. While these occur, you should strive to identify them, as well as the subsequent signs, and set your determination to blend them with your spiritual practice. When the all-empty clear light dawns, you should recall your understanding of your previous view of the Middle Way[99] while placing your mind single-pointedly upon the union of bliss and emptiness to the best

---

99. This means your view of the Madhyamaka that you established prior to death.

of your ability. If you are able to mix the clear light of death [with the truth body] after recognizing it, you will subsequently be able to recognize the intermediate state; therefore, the best means of recognizing the intermediate state is to be able to mix the clear light of death. When you begin to emerge from that clear light, through the force of your previous determination and familiarity, you will at least be able to meditate on yourself as the yidam deity through imagination. It is at this point that the intermediate state begins to appear.

You should contemplate that "nothing whatsoever is ultimately established," continue with your view of suchness, and meditate on how all worlds and beings are like illusions.

How to Meditate on the Clear Light has two sections:

1. How to Meditate on the Clear Light while Awake
2. How to Meditate on the Clear Light while Sleeping

How to Meditate on the Clear Light while Awake

In general, there are several types of clear light. There are the common and uncommon clear lights, the objective and subjective clear lights, and the hidden meaning and ultimate clear lights. The objective clear light is the emptiness of all phenomena being free from the extremes of permanence and annihilation. The subjective clear light is the mind of a person realizing [the objective clear light]. These are common to both the Hinayana and Mahayana and all four classes of tantra, and are referred to [collectively] as "the general meaning clear light." The uncommon clear light is the realization of suchness of the objective clear light through the subjective [mind of] simultaneously born great bliss and is a unique feature of highest yoga tantra. The clear light of highest yoga tantra has the basis, path, and result. Therefore, the basis clear light is the clear light during sleep and during death, so it is something possessed by each and every ordinary being; however, they do not recognize it [when it manifests]. The example and the meaning clear lights are the clear lights of the path and are referred to as "the hidden meaning clear lights." For example clear light, there are both similitude [example clear light] and actual [example clear light].[100] For meaning clear light, there is the clear light of either the fourth or the fifth stage.[101] The ultimate clear light is unique to union. The clear light of ultimate meaning is that of learning and no-more-learning. For that reason, meaning clear light is the primary subject matter of highest yoga tantra, while example clear light is secondary. The similitude of the illusory body is accomplished through example clear light, and the actual illusory body is accomplished through meaning clear light. The clear light manifests easily during the day through meditating on inner fire at the heart.[102]

With respect to the actual practice, meditate on a blue syllable HUM upon a moon seat within the central channel at the heart of yourself visualized as the deity, from which light rays radiate, cleansing the impurities of all worlds and beings [and] creating only limitless purity. Again, all worlds, as the container, dissolve into all living beings, as the contents. They [i.e., all beings] [then] also dissolve into you, and [you yourself visualized as the deity body] dissolve upward from the soles of your feet and downward from the crown of your head, and once it [i.e., your body] dissolves into the shabgyu of the HUM upon the moon seat at your heart, it continues upward to the nada, and the nada that is within the central channel at your heart is also absorbed into unobservable emptiness. While remaining within that state, the winds enter, abide in, and dissolve into your heart as you progress through the four empties, whereby the clear light dawns. At that point, the red and white elements have collected within your heart, whereby the four joys manifest, and once you unify bliss and emptiness, you should meditate single-pointedly. That bliss and

100. A similitude example clear light is when the winds enter the central channel somewhere other than the heart channel wheel. The actual example clear light is when the winds enter the central channel at the heart. The ultimate example clear light is when *all* the winds enter the indestructible drop within the heart channel wheel. "Similitude" and "actual" can also refer to example and meaning clear light, respectively.

101. There are five stages of the completion stage according to the structure set out in the teachings of Guhyasamaja: (1) isolated speech, (2) isolated mind, (3) illusory body, (4) clear light, and (5) union. The clear light of stage three is the ultimate example clear light, the clear light of stage four is meaning clear light, and stage five is the union of the meaning clear light and the pure illusory body. Stage five also contains a division of the union of learning and the union of no-more-learning, the latter being synonymous with enlightenment.

102. Here the term "inner fire" is being used to reference completion-stage practices in general within the framework of the Six Yogas of Naropa.

emptiness functions as the actual antidote to the delusion-obstructions and marks the attainment of meaning clear light.

As you begin to arise from the clear light, in the first instant you are propelled to arise in the illusory body of Vajrayogini in that very place within your heart. In the second instant you transfer to a location separate from your old aggregates. In Je [Tsongkhapa's] text, he states that there is a sun seat for the HUM at your heart, yet it doesn't matter whether it's a moon or sun. Therefore, since it might cause confusion [to use a sun seat] at this point, you should meditate as [explained] earlier and use a moon. It also makes no difference whether you use the guru-deity, drop, or syllable [as the object at your heart].

How to Meditate on the Clear Light while Sleeping

Once you meditate on going for refuge, generating bodhichitta, and guru yoga during the day, you should make offerings and praises as well as powerful supplications to apprehend the clear light of sleep. The *Hevajra Tantra* states,

> The simultaneously born is not proclaimed by others,
> And you will not find it anywhere [else].
> The time and method are taught by the guru,
> And should be understood through his merit.

Je [Losang] Chökyi Gyaltsen proclaimed,

> The exalted wisdom of great bliss is not proclaimed by others,
> And is not found anywhere else;
> It is directly realized through serving you
> And hearing your teachings; your kindness is incomparable.

Initially, your sleep is very dense and deep, making it difficult to apprehend the clear light. Later, if [your sleep is too light and] you wish to have a deep sleep to apprehend [the clear light], you should rely on nutritious food by eating oily food, tsampa and butter, and so forth. Dress warmly and take only naps for a day or so. Next, when lying down, put your head to the north, your back to the east, face west, and place your feet in the south—or imagine it—while lying in the lion posture. Set your determination to apprehend the clear light of sleep before dreams arise.[103] Once you unmistakably focus your mind upon the bluish-black syllable HUM upon a moon seat within the central channel at the heart of yourself appearing clearly as the deity, you should perform the stages of subsequent destruction as explained earlier, whereby the winds enter, abide in, and dissolve into your central channel, causing the four signs— such as the mirage-like [appearance] and so forth—to arise in sequence. After this, the "empty" of the path of white appearance will manifest. Next, the "very empty" of the path of red increase will manifest. Next, the "great empty" of the path of black near-attainment will manifest; the upper portion of this has mindfulness, after which you will progress to utter darkness without mindfulness. To whatever degree your mindful-ness deteriorates, [this] is the degree to which it will later transform into the stability of the clear light; therefore it is not a fault.[104]

Next, once you awaken from the pitch-black unconsciousness, there arises an appearance that is just like the natural color of the sky, which is free from the obscurations of contaminants of moonlight, sunlight, or darkness and similar to the natural color of the pure sky at dawn. This is called "the all-empty clear light." You should remain in that state for as long as you possibly can.

Regarding the meaning of [inducing] deep sleep, if you awaken because of sleeping lightly or if numerous dreams appear, [then] even though you awaken, do not open your eyes. Instead, visualize the syllable HUM at the heart of yourself as the deity and dissolve your body into the syllable HUM. That also sequentially dissolves from the shabgyu upward, as before, and collects into the state of unobservable [emptiness]. This is the stage of "holding the body entirely."[105] If dreams arise, you should also recall the deity and syllable, sequentially withdraw properly, and go back to sleep.

103. This is because the clear light manifests prior to the actual dream state.
104. This means that the length and stability of the clear light are determined by the length of time spent in the unconscious period of the mind of black near-attainment; therefore it is something desirable.
105. There are two concentrations of sequential dissolution: that of "subsequent destruction" and "holding the body entirely." The first has already been explained; this is when you visualize light rays radiating from your heart and pervading the universe, which are then sequentially

These four empties are also related to the four joys. The all-empty clear light is related to supreme simultaneously born joy. Therefore, although there is bliss in relation to the nonconceptual mind, those two are only similar in being labeled "bliss," and they are not at all similar in meaning.[106] In that way, once you have cultivated simultaneously born great bliss and recalled the view of the Middle Way through a definite conclusion about the meaning of suchness, you should seize it with an unwavering mind. This is called "the inseparable bliss and emptiness of highest yoga Mantra." [With respect to the two types of bliss], there are many who mistake what is dissimilar as being the similar; therefore, you should make a careful distinction.[107]

Next, with respect to the ability to continue your concentration during sleep: if you don't apprehend the clear light through the force of wind, [then] the three empties will not arise prior to the clear light—and with the exception of a mere portion that is similar to the signs, such as mirage-like [appearance] and so forth, which may arise prior to the first empty, their sequence will not emerge in the proper order. Therefore, the unerring sequence of the signs and the three empties will not arise prior to the concentration of [the clear light of] sleep, and the clear light will lack clarity and radiance. Thus, you should place your mind in a state of meditative equipoise on the clear light to the best of your ability, and if you are unable to accomplish that, you should utilize the special techniques for arising [as the deity] in the dream state, as explained earlier during the section on mixing during sleep.

---

dissolved into your heart and into the clear light. "Holding the body entirely" is when you merely withdraw the body and leave the outer environment.

106. This means that although the term "bliss" is used in relation to the mind of nonconceptuality, it is utterly unlike the simultaneously born bliss that comes from causing the winds to enter, abide in, and dissolve into the central channel.

107. This means that there are those who mistake other types of bliss, such as that aroused from the state of nonconceptuality or even the bliss of tranquil abiding, to be the simultaneously born bliss that is aroused through causing the winds to enter, abide in, and dissolve into the central channel, yet the latter is vastly superior in numerous ways.

Transference of Consciousness and Insertion of Consciousness as Limbs of the Path has two sections:

1. TRANSFERENCE OF CONSCIOUSNESS TO A HIGHER REALM
2. INSERTION OF CONSCIOUSNESS

Transference of Consciousness to a Higher Realm

The term "transference of consciousness" means migrating to an increasingly higher physical basis. If in your next life you are born as something like an animal, that life form will interrupt your meditation on the path. Therefore you should attain a physical basis for practicing the path [through the practice of transference of consciousness], which is why this is also well known as the "shortcut path." Regarding the benefits of this path, the *Vajradaka Tantra*[108] states,

> Those who engage in killing a brahman every day,
> Performing the five actions of immediate retribution,
> Stealing, pillaging, and even rape,
> Will be liberated through this path.
> You will not be defiled by these nonvirtues
> And will far transcend the faults of samsara.

Being purified and liberated means that you are liberated from the lower realms and that you are purifying the negative karma that would cause rebirth there. The time for engaging in transference of consciousness is expressed in the *Vajradaka Tantra* when it states,

> Perform transference when the time comes.
> The wrong time becomes killing the deities.
> By simply killing the deities
> You will burn in hell.

This is stating that because you are visualizing yourself as the deity, if you

---

108. Tib. *rDo rje mkha' gro.*

perform transference of consciousness at the wrong time, it is killing a deity; therefore it is stated,

> The aggregates are the nature of the five buddhas;
> To despise them is the eighth [downfall].

Thus, if you have tantric vows, [premature transference of consciousness] is a grave fault and becomes the eighth root downfall; therefore, you will go to hell and so forth. It is for these reasons that you should understand the [appropriate] time. For that, you should be skilled in the signs of death, and if you see the signs of death, you should employ the means of reversing [your impending death] with rituals such as "deceiving death"[109] and so forth. If even those don't overcome [the signs of impending death], you should [begin training] in transference of consciousness at least six months beforehand, and before you are affected with illnesses such as an infectious disease.[110]

Regarding the special practice of transference of consciousness, our text states that you should be able to properly collect the winds through meditation on inner fire and vase breathing. As a preliminary to this practice, it is acceptable to practice according to preliminaries to the Six Yogas, in which case they should be done at the point of practicing mental recitation.[111] Next, you should meditate on the body as an empty shell for a few moments. Visualize the three channels as before. The central channel is the size of an arrow shaft with its upper end reaching the Brahma aperture. There is a white inverted KSHA syllable blocking the hole. The channel wheels at the navel and heart are visualized as before. The lower end of the three channels reach four finger-widths below the navel, where the right and left channels enter the central channel. Visualize the short AH, as before, upon a moon seat within the central channel at the navel channel wheel. In the center of your heart channel wheel is the life-

---

109. Tib. *'chi slu.*

110. This is because if you wait until you are gravely ill before training in the transference of consciousness, you will most likely be too ill to train effectively enough to actualize the appropriate results. Therefore, you should train while you are well, gain some experience, and then implement your practice of transference of consciousness at the time of death.

111. This is in reference to the mental recitation section of the Vajrayogini sadhana.

supporting wind like a moon split in two, and the cut face of the half-moon shape is facing downward and is the size of a pea. Above that, in the center of the bulge [of the half-moon's convex curve], is a moon seat, upon which is a long inverted HUM. At the tip of the nada of the HUM is an inverted syllable HI. In the shabgyu is an inverted KA. Between the HI and KA is the HUM, appearing like a reflection in a mirror. You should absorb your mind into it and remain there.

Next, you restrain the winds and bring the winds from the right and left channels into the central channel. Imagine that they strike the short AH as the lower winds are drawn upward and ignite the short AH. When striking it with the winds, [the short AH] pushes against the life-supporting wind at your heart, whereby [the HUM] is as though a cloth bag is turned inside out, [filling the HUM like a parachute,] and the [HUM] syllable also changes so that it is facing upright, after which you imagine that it moves upward and pushes against the syllable KSHA at your crown, causing it to move slightly. Restrain the winds once again, whereby the life-supporting wind together with the [short AH] syllable revert to their inverted position at your heart. You should repeat the process of sending the wind upward and so forth. In this way, sincerely apply yourself in four sessions. You should continue training until you receive signs such as itching on the crown of your head, a blister, swelling, and so forth.

With respect to applying the action,[112] you should block the eight doors: (1) the mouth, (2) navel, (3) sex organ, (4) anus, (5) point between the eyebrows, (6) nose, (7) eyes, and (8) ears. If we follow the advice of Yongzin Pandita the Great,[113] he suggests that beginners meditate properly on the central channel and then practice transference of consciousness within the central channel. If you practice in that way, it is also acceptable if you don't block the doors of the senses. Such a practitioner should give away his or her belongings. Sit in the squatting position [with your arms wrapped around your two knees]. Visualize Vajrayogini on the crown of your head, inseparable from your guru, with her two legs on your two

112. Tib. *las la sbyar ba*. This refers to applying the practice at the time of death.
113. Yongzin Pandita was the reincarnation of Kanchen Yeshe Gyaltsen (see note 14 above). Unfortunately I was unable to obtain his text.

shoulders standing above you, so that her bhaga[114] is directly aligned with your crown aperture. Invoke the guru-deity and absorb her. Surrounding her are a retinue of heroes and dakinis to whom you should make offerings and extremely powerful supplications. Next, light rays radiate from the BAM at her heart and illuminate the syllable KSHA at your crown aperture, after which they dissolve into the syllable BAM at her heart. Each time you bring the winds into embrace with the vase breath, your mind absorbs into the short AH, and you focus on it single-pointedly. Red, hook-like light rays emerge from [Vajrayogini's] heart, move through your central channel, and strike the short AH. Simultaneously, you recite "EE HIK," and the light rays draw the short AH up to your throat. As you recite it again, it arrives at your crown, and the syllables HUM and so forth dissolve into the life-supporting wind. As you recite "EE HIK" again, imagine that the life-supporting wind dissolves into the life-supporting wind at [Vajrayogini's heart] as the syllable BAM. Thus, until your last breath, you should not let it descend but only raise it upward.

Insertion of Consciousness

Because the consciousness of another person vacates his [or her] body when he dies, and your consciousness enters that corpse, it is called "insertion of consciousness."[115] These instructions are unique to highest yoga tantra and are taught extensively in mother tantra as well as in a few instances of father tantra.

As for the physical basis of the person who will be undertaking the practice, he has trained his mental continuum in the common path; has obtained the complete empowerment and has been perfectly protecting his commitments and vows while training in the generation stage through four daily sessions; has been trained in the entering, abiding, and dissolving of the winds in the central channel through the completion stage, and through summoning the life-supporting wind of the heart through vase

114. *Bhaga* is a Sanskrit word used honorifically in tantric texts to refer to the vagina of a karma mudra. Another term often used is "secret lotus," or simply "lotus."
115. The Tibetan term *grong 'jug* literally means "entering a corpse"; however, because of the macabre sense it brings, I have opted to use translator Voula Zarpani's term "insertion of consciousness."

breathing and the heat of inner fire; [and] has become capable of expelling his consciousness from the center of the red and white elements. Regarding its necessity, there are three [main reasons]: (1) if you are of low social status, you won't be able to accomplish great works for the welfare of others; (2) if you are afflicted with a chronic disease, you won't be able to accomplish the welfare of others; and (3) if you are extremely old, you will not be able to make progress on the path; therefore, you need to assume a new physical basis that is of good lineage, free from illness, and so forth.

With respect to the practice, having established the boundaries [for your practice], you should present offerings and tormas to the guru and deity and then make supplications. Once you present offerings to the dakinis and Dharma protectors, you should entrust them with the performance of their enlightened actions. Set up a square, black platform within the retreat house, upon which is placed a fully qualified skull cup, on the bottom of which is a syllable HUM written clearly with a medicinal stone.[116] Set the skull cup with its forehead facing forward, as though you and it are embracing each other. You should sincerely apply yourself to the practice of the seven-limbed prayer and so forth while being endowed with the yoga of yourself as the deity. Next, within the central channel at your heart is a blue syllable HUM, which your mind enters into and remains focused on. From within that state, for the sake of drawing the winds from the right nostril, you correlate its movement and imagine that [the blue HUM] emerges from your right nostril and dissolves into the HUM within the skull cup. Remain in that state for as long as possible without inhaling. When you are unable [to remain in a state of exhalation], inhale slowly. Again, exhale and imagine that the [blue] HUM exits through your [right] nostril and dissolves into the HUM [within the skull cup], as before. Through repeatedly training in this way, signs will emerge, such as the skull cup becoming warm, trembling, making sounds of life, and so forth.

After these initial signs of success, wash the fresh corpse of a human being or animal that does not have any wounds. Adorned with pleasing ornaments, [set the corpse] so that it is sitting face to face with you, and if

116. Tib. *rdo rgyus*.

it is the corpse of an animal, lay it on its right side. Visualize both yourself and the corpse as the deity, and imagine a syllable HUM at both of your hearts. As before, simultaneously with your exhalation, your mind as the syllable HUM emerges, enters the left nostril of the corpse, and dissolves into the HUM at its heart. Hold that for as long as you are able and so forth, as before. Practice this repeatedly until the corpse begins breathing, and an aroma and warmth return.

When this happens, find a new corpse of a good lineage that did not die of some infectious disease and is not decayed or afflicted with smallpox or any other such faults. Wash it well, adorn it with ornaments, and make powerful supplications and entrust [the divinities] with [the performance of their] enlightened actions. You should employ the services of an assistant with pure commitments who is skilled in [ritual] actions. Forsake conceptions of your body as being ordinary, and with the understanding that all phenomena that appear in samsara are like illusions, you and the corpse sit facing each other. Visualize a syllable HUM at the hearts of both of you, visualized as the deity as before. Simultaneously with the exhalation, your mind as the syllable HUM emerges from your right nostril, enters the left nostril of the corpse, and dissolves into the HUM at its heart. Exhale strongly without inhaling, and hold it there.

Next, when your new aggregates come to life, your assistant should feed you and care for you, saying, "I will look after you," and until you attain stability it is essential that you keep your old aggregates hidden. Next, when you attain some stability, as a way of repaying the kindness of your old aggregates, you offer [your body] to the cremation pyre and make clay votives of enlightened beings with its ashes. With your new-found stability, you should progress through the higher spiritual paths and work for the welfare of the teachings and living beings. This [method of insertion of consciousness] finds its source in the tantras and Indian texts, where they explain it without the need for such hardships. The teaching in this text is in accordance with Je [Tsongkhapa's] commentary and was composed in accordance with the practice tradition of the former gurus. Although you leave your body prematurely, the faults of [thereby] killing a deity and so forth are not taught [as in the transference of consciousness]. Since you are not entering your new aggregates through the force of a fully qualified samsaric death, it is not a fully qualified samsaric rebirth. Instead, your consciousness moves directly between the two [collections of aggregates]; therefore, it is also not a fully qualified intermediate state of existence. For that reason, although you abandon your former body, your recollection of the Dharma from your previous body does not deteriorate.

How to Perform the Tantric Activities for Enhancing the Path

In general, there are three types of conduct [each corresponding to a type of person] for those engaging in tantric practice: (1) the types of conduct free of attachment are the tantric activity for a person of lesser aspiration; (2) the types of activity of persons of vast aspiration, who practice according to the grounds and perfections; and (3) persons of profound and superior aspiration, who practice the tantric activity with attachment. For the third, there are two activities: (1) the conduct of the generation stage, and (2) the conduct of the completion stage. For each of those, there are also three activities: (1) with elaboration, (2) without elaboration, and (3) completely without elaboration. Someone who has perfected the gross and subtle generation stage does not need to engage in the tantric activities to accomplish the activities of peace and so forth, nor does he [or she] need to accomplish the attainments of the eight great attainments.[117] However, for those eight you must apply mere concentration for a period of seven days and so forth, whereby they will quickly be accomplished. Regarding the tantric activities with elaboration and with-

---

117. The eight great attainments are (1) sword, (2) pill, (3) eye lotion, (4) swift-footedness, (5) alchemy, (6) flight, (7) invisibility, and (8) going underground. However, Ngulchu Dharmabhadra's *Roar of Thunder*, p. 133, lists them as follows: "With the sword attainment, if you merely hold the sword in your hand, you will arrive wherever you wish. With the pill attainment, through eating a [blessed] pill, you will become strong, radiant, and glowing. With the eye medicine attainment, by applying the eye medicine, you will be able to see treasures under the ground. The swift-footedness attainment is called by many 'the leaf of swift-footedness,' whereby mounting that [leaf], you arrive wherever you desire. With the invisibility attainment, you smear a substance [on your body], whereby others will be unable to see you. With the elixir attainment, as soon as you eat an elixir pill, an old person eighty years of age becomes youthful again. With the Kechari attainment, you are able to go to Dakini Land without abandoning your body. With the underground attainment, you are able to go underground, like a fish in water. These are the eight attainments."

out elaboration, they are tantric activities utilizing enjoyments, through understanding the nature of suchness in conjunction with the objects of desire in general, and a knowledge-woman of desire in particular. For the tantric activity with elaboration, you assemble numerous male and female practitioners and engage in great elaborations, such as the use of costumes, singing and dancing, and so forth. The tantric activity without elaboration is practiced in a concise way, with merely yourself and one karma mudra without any other elaborations. In the tantric activity completely without elaboration, you don't rely upon a karma mudra and instead utilize merely a wisdom mudra and do nothing more than eat, sleep, and defecate.[118] These [practitioners] spend most of their time sleeping and practice the rounds of mixing during sleep.

Regarding the person engaging in the tantric activities with the completion stage, there are three occasions when he [or she] practices the tantric activities: (1) once he attains a similitude of isolated mind and is on the brink of attaining the illusory body through example clear light, (2) once he accomplishes the illusory [body] and is about to accomplish meaning clear light of the fourth stage, and (3) for the sake of accomplishing the union of no-more-learning once he has attained the union of learning.

Actualizing the Result

Furthermore, once you simultaneously abandon the delusion-obstructions together with their seeds through meaning clear light, you arise from that clear light and accomplish the pure illusory body. This is the union of learning. The mind of meaning clear light that you have while in the meditative equipoise of the union of learning is the "union of realization." However, when it becomes necessary to arise from that clear light in subsequent attainment, you have the "union of abandonment." With that union of learning, you progress to the sequential [abandonment] of the nine rounds of obstructions to omniscience. That concentration is called the "concentration migrating to glory." Next, at dusk you offer a tsok

---

118. These types of practitioners are referred to as *kusali*. They keep their attainments hidden and primarily practice the clear light of sleep.

LAMA TSONGKHAPA

offering (ganachakra) to your guru and request instructions [on attaining enlightenment]. Through your meditative equipoise in the third period of the day, you [continue] until dawn and attain the vajra-like concentration. In the first instance, you abandon the most subtle obscurations to omniscience, which is the actual antidote to mistaken dualistic appearances and their imprints, and you actualize the final mind of the truth body. In the second instant, the union of learning transforms into the state of the union of no-more-learning and you attain enlightenment.

That second [enlightened] body will remain unwaveringly for as long as samsara exists. Such a state possesses two purities: (1) there is the objective clear light, which is the uncompounded truth body and is the actual exalted wisdom of omniscience, and (2) there is the subjective clear light, which is truth body of exalted wisdom and is called the "body of great bliss" and is the exalted wisdom of omniscience that perceives the multiplicity of [all] things. That truth body of exalted wisdom is a body that is the support for the form body that is the complete enjoyment body accomplished from mere wind and mind; those two bodies are what is referred to as "one entity and different isolates."[119] In that way, that body of union will emanate limitless emanations, such as bodies of supreme emanation and so forth, and those two form bodies [i.e., the enjoyment and emanation bodies] will work in immeasurable ways for the welfare of living beings for as long as samsara exists.

This [work was based on] two texts that are similar to the notes called *The Former and Latter Fundamental Treatise*,[120] said to have been composed by Marpa. Regarding the source of the [teachings] on inner fire, [they] come from Krishnacharya, who is called "Acharya," who in turn transmitted them in four transmissions to Tilopa, and are called the *Spring*

---

119. In Tibetan Buddhist philosophy, something is said to be a single entity with different conceptual isolates when it can appear to a conceptual consciousness with two different names or attributes. In some cases, the two isolates are equivalent and mutually inclusive, as in the case of two synonyms, for example, padma and lotus. In other cases, they are mutually exclusive and nonequivalent, as when the Prasangika Madhyamaka school argues that the table and its emptiness (its lack of inherent existence) are two isolates that are mutually opposed yet are both within a single entity. For more on the two truths, see Jeffrey Hopkins, *Meditation on Emptiness* (New York: Wisdom, 2024), p. 414; and Guy Newland, *The Two Truths* (Ithaca, NY: Snow Lion Publications, 1992), and also his *Appearance and Reality: The Two Truths in Four Buddhist Systems* (Ithaca, NY: Snow Lion Publications, 1999), pp. 75–93.

120. Tib. *Ka dpe snga ma dang phyi ma.*

Drop of Krishnacharya[121] and the *Spring Drop of Samputa.*[122] Regarding the term "spring," this is in reference to *vasanta* of the heart; as for "drop," this is the *tilaka* of the red element at the navel.[123] In dependence upon the inner fire, the spring and the drop are united whereby you generate bliss, and [this] is therefore called "spring drop." Regarding the Arya tradition of Guhyasamaja, such as Nagarjuna's composition *The Five Stages* and so forth, these were Marpa's source for the lineages of the illusory body and clear light, which is in accordance with Je Marpa's statement, "I remained in the land of Nepal for three years," and so forth. The transference of consciousness and insertion of consciousness rely upon the *Four Vajra Seats Tantra*. It is for these reasons that Je [Tsongkhapa] entitled his text *Endowed with the Three Inspirations*. As it is a most wondrous and eloquent explanation endowed with these three [reliable sources],[124] it is worthy of our trust.

Now I will explain a little about your daily Dharma practice. You should continually meditate on inner fire in either an extensive or concise fashion. With respect to practicing transference of consciousness, you should practice for a period of time, such as seven days, until signs [of success] arise, after which you shouldn't practice it too much and instead do just enough to not forget [how to do it properly]. During those times, you should amend the eleven yogas of [the Vajrayogini practice of] Naro Kachö with the fourteen essential topics explained in the *Heruka Root Tantra.*[125] Alternatively, you can practice the concise eleven yogas of Vajrayogini. It is also acceptable to use the [Vajrayogini] self-generation that is only one page long. It is also acceptable to practice any of the extensive or concise yogas of Vajrabhairava or Heruka Chakrasamvara.

Thus you should formulate an excellent understanding of the stages for

---

121. Tib. *Nag po spyod pa'i dpyid thig.*
122. Tib. *Sambhuta'i dpyid thig.*
123. In this sentence, vasanta and tilaka are Sanskrit terms for "spring" and "drop," respectively.
124. These three reliable sources that inspired Tsongkhapa are (1) the inner fire systems stemming from Krishnacharya, (2) the illusory body and clear lights of the Arya tradition of Guhyasamaja as taught by Nagarjuna and brought to Tibet by Marpa, and (3) the transference of consciousness stemming from *Four Vajra Seats Tantra*.
125. For a translation of the *Heruka Root Tantra*, see David Gonsalez, trans., *The Chakrasamvara Root Tantra* (Somerville, MA: Wisdom Publications, 2020).

progressing on the common and uncommon paths and make the practices of the higher paths the objects of your prayers.

The cycle of teachings for a person of small scope reveals the means for overcoming your craving for the things of this life and next. The cycle of teachings of the person of intermediate scope reveals the means of overcoming attachment to all of samsara. The cycle of teachings of the person of great scope reveals the means of generating the mind of enlightenment rooted in love and compassion. These should be the heart of your practice. In addition to that, you should extract the essence of this life of leisure by sincerely applying yourself to the generation stage and the lower stages of the completion stage.

Colophon

Adityabandhu[126] amid the guides of India,
The moon amid the constellations,
The mountain of jewels amid the earth—
Amid the scholars and siddhas you are called "Dharma[bhadra]."

Although there are numerous trees covering this earth,
Rare is the wish-fulfilling tree that bestows all wishes.
In the same way, although there are countless beings of great renown,
Rare are those who are the treasury of qualities of scripture and
    realization.

This teaching does not come from the melodious song of
Sarasvati or the flute of a gandharva.
They are limitless teachings of pleasant words and profound meaning;
I was so fortunate to have received such nectar.

Therefore, to refresh my memory and
To benefit others of similar fortune,
I have clearly set forth a few sections of such teachings
By composing whatever I could remember through the efforts of
    my three doors.

The perfections attained through efforts in this method
Are like emulating the full autumn moon free of clouds,
Whereby self and other are liberated from the vast sphere of two
    obscurations
And blossom as the supreme garden of the three bodies.

These notes on the profound path of the Six Yogas of Naropa entitled *Adorning the True Intent of the [Three] Inspirations*, were repeatedly
requested for a long time from our teacher of incomparable kindness whose name, "The Great Scholar and Siddha Jetsun [Ngulchu]

---

126. This is another name of Buddha Shakyamuni.

Dharmabhadra Palsangpo," is difficult to say.[127] These days, these profound instructions are extremely rare within the Yellow Hat tradition in the Land of Snow. Through his kindness this profound commentary was taught for private and public [disciples alike] to benefit the teachings and beings, beginning from the third day of the eleventh month of the Water Tiger Year [1842] and lasting for seven days. The notes were inscribed by Je Trung Tsering.

SHUBHA MASTU

During the carving of woodblocks in the Fire Pig Year [1887], I noticed numerous errors in the two prototype manuscripts; therefore the illuminator of the teachings of the Yellow Hats, Je Trung Rinpoche Losang Tenzin, the supreme holder of the teaching, examined it in detail, and through his editing made numerous corrections. The teachings were once again edited by Yangchen Drupai Dorje; however, they were not ready for the woodblock carver by the Fire Pig Year. In accordance with astrological calculation, in the Earth Bird Year [1888] I had to go to another region; therefore they were not carved. Once again, for the sake of accomplishing the wish to carve them in the second month of the Earth Bird Year, the sole heart disciple of our supreme guide, the Maha Pandita, Jetsun Lama Yangchen Drupai Dorje Palsangpo, out of his great kindness perfectly composed the first seven pages.

---

127. The phrase "So and so, whose name is difficult to say" is an honorific expression used by disciples when referring to their gurus who have passed away.

Outline of the Text

Explaining the Precepts for the Profound Path of the Six Yogas of Naropa has two sections:
1. The Preliminary Meditations That Are the Basis for This Path (19–31)
2. How to Meditate upon this Path on That Basis (31–95)

The Preliminary Meditations That Are the Basis for This Path has two sections:
1. The Initial Preliminaries of the Common Mahayana Path (19–24)
2. The Uncommon Preliminaries of Highest Yoga Tantra (24–31)

The Initial Preliminaries of the Common Mahayana Path has two sections:
1. Revealing the Necessity for the Disciples of This Tradition to Also Train Their Minds in the Common Path (20)
2. Sequentially Training the Mind in That Path (21–24)

The Uncommon Preliminaries of Highest Yoga Tantra has two sections:
1. The General Preliminaries (24–27)
2. The Special Preliminaries (27–31)

The General Preliminaries has two sections:
1. Revealing the Necessity of Obtaining the Complete Empowerment (25–26)
2. Revealing the Necessity of Protecting Your Commitments (26–27)

The Special Preliminaries has two sections:
1. Purifying Negative Karma and Obscurations through Vajra-sattva Meditation and Recitation (28–29)
2. Receiving Blessing by Worshiping through Guru Yoga (29–31)

Receiving Blessing by Worshiping through Guru Yoga has two sections:
1. Meditating on the Guru in the Field of Merit (29–30)
2. Making Supplications after Presenting Offerings to Him (30–31)

How to Meditate upon This Path on That Basis has two sections:
1. Meditation on the Generation Stage (31–32)
2. Meditation on the Completion Stage (32–95)

Meditation on the Completion Stage has three sections:
1. The Mode of Existence of the Basis (32–35)
2. The Stages for Progressing on the Path (35–91)
3. The Way of Actualizing the Result (91–95)

The Mode of Existence of the Basis has two sections:
1. The Mode of Existence of the Mind (32–35)
2. The Mode of Existence of the Body (35)

The Stages for Progressing on the Path has two sections:
1. The Six Magical Wheels and Meditating on the Body as an Empty Shell (36–40)
2. The Stages of Meditating on the Actual Path (40–91)

The Six Magical Wheels and Meditating on the Body as an Empty Shell has two sections:
1. How to Perform the Physical Exercises from the Famed Six Magical Wheels of Naropa (36–39)
2. Meditating on the Body as an Empty Shell (39–40)

How to Perform the Physical Exercises from the Famed Six Magical Wheels of Naropa has six sections:
1. Filling Like a Vase (37)
2. Turning Like a Wheel (37–38)
3. Hooking Like a Hook (38)
4. Raising the Vajra-Binding Mudra in the Sky and Casting It Downward (38)
5. Straightening the Body Like a Female Dog Dry Heaving Forcefully (39)
6. Shaking the Head and Body and Flexing the Joints (39)

The Stages of Meditating on the Actual Path has two sections:
1. The Way of Structuring the Path (40–41)
2. The Stages of Being Guided on the Path (41–95)

The Stages of Being Guided on the Path has two sections:
1. The Meaning of Being Guided along the Path (42–90)
2. How to Perform the Tantric Activities for Enhancing the Path (90–91)

The Meaning of Being Guided along the Path has two sections:
1. The Meaning of the Actual Path (42–83)
2. Transference of Consciousness and Insertion of Consciousness as Limbs of the Path (84–90)

The Meaning of the Actual Path has two sections:
1. Generating the Four Joys by Drawing the Winds into the Central Channel (42–60)
2. How to Meditate on the Illusory Body and the Clear Light in Dependence upon That (60–83)

Generating the Four Joys by Drawing the Winds into the Central Channel has two sections:
1. Meditating on the Inner Condition of Inner Fire (42–58)
2. Meditating in Dependence upon a Karma Mudra as the Outer Condition (58–60)

Meditating on the Inner Condition of Inner Fire has two sections:
1. Absorbing the Winds into the Central Channel through Meditation on Inner Fire (42–52)
2. How to Generate the Four Joys in Dependence upon Collecting [the Winds] (52–58)

Absorbing the Winds into the Central Channel through Meditation on Inner Fire has two sections:
1. How to Meditate on Inner Fire (42–50)
2. How to Cause the Winds to Enter, Abide in, and Dissolve into the Central Channel through Meditating in This Way (51–52)

How to Meditate on Inner Fire has three sections:
1. Meditation through Visualizing the Channels (43–45)
2. Meditation through Visualizing the Syllables (46–47)
3. How to Meditate on the Vase Breathing of Wind (47–50)

How to Cause the Winds to Enter, Abide in, and Dissolve into the Central Channel through Meditating in This Way (51–52)

How to Generate the Four Joys in Dependence upon Such Entering has three sections:
1. How to Manifest the Signs and [Cause] the Inner Fire to Blaze (53–54)
2. How to Generate the Four Joys in Dependence upon Melting the Bodhichitta (54–57)
3. How to Meditate on Simultaneously Born Exalted Wisdom (57–58)

How to Meditate on the Illusory Body and the Clear Light in Dependence upon That has two sections:
1. A General Presentation of How to Meditate on the Remaining Paths in Dependence upon Inner Fire (60–66)
2. How to Meditate on the Individual Paths (66–83)

How to Meditate on the Individual Paths has two sections:
1. How to Meditate on the Illusory Body (67–79)
2. How to Meditate on the Clear Light (79–83)

How to Meditate on the Illusory Body has three sections:
1. How to Meditate on Appearances as Illusory (67–68)
2. How to Meditate on Dreams as Illusory (68–72)
3. How to Meditate on the Intermediate State as Illusory (73–79)

How to Meditate on Dreams as Illusory has four sections:
1. Apprehending Dreams (68–70)
2. Purifying and Increasing (70–71)
3. Abandoning Fear and Training in the Illusory (71–72)
4. Meditating on the Suchness of Dreams (72)

How to Meditate on the Intermediate State as Illusory has two sections:
1. Presenting the General Thesis of the Intermediate State (73–76)
2. Presenting the Stages of Practice (77–79)

How to Meditate on the Clear Light has two sections:
1. How to Meditate on the Clear Light while Awake (79–81)
2. How to Meditate on the Clear Light while Sleeping (81–83)

Transference of Consciousness and Insertion of Consciousness as Limbs of the Path has two sections:
1. Transference of Consciousness to a Higher Realm (84–87)
2. Insertion of Consciousness (87–90)

How to Perform the Tantric Activities for Enhancing the Path (90–91)

Actualizing the Result (91–95)

Colophon (96–97)

Panchen Losang Chökyi Gyaltsen

PART 2

Commentary on the First Panchen Lama's Prayer for Liberation from Fear in the Intermediate State

A Commentary on Liberation from Fear of the
Perilous Journey of the Intermediate State Entitled
"Adorning the True Intent of the [First] Panchen [Lama]"

(Bar do 'phrang sgrol gyi gsol 'debs 'jigs sgrol gyi dpa' bo'i rnam bshad
pan chen dgongs rgyan)

NAMO GURU MANJUGOSHA

The three bodies of powerful pervasive Lord Vajradhara appear as
An actor in saffron robes endowed with the three trainings;
Tsongkhapa, the guru of all beings in the three realms,
May I always be protected by the auspiciousness of your three secrets.

I bow to the feet of Losang Chökyi Gyaltsen.
Please sit on the hundred anthers of the lotus of my heart.
Through my intelligence I shall loosen the knots of your
Eloquent and wonderful explanation that is difficult to understand.

Furthermore, this explanation of Panchen Losang Chökyi Gyaltsen's composition entitled *A Hero Liberated from Fear: A Supplication for Liberation from Fear of the Perilous Journey of the Intermediate State* has three sections:

1. THE MEANING OF THE OPENING LINE OF THE COMPOSITION
2. THE MEANING OF THE SUBJECT MATTER OF THE COMPOSITION
3. THE MEANING OF THE CONCLUSION OF THE COMPOSITION

The Meaning of the Opening Line of the Composition

The opening line of homage states:

NAMO GURU MANJUGOSHA YA

Namo means "prostrate" or "bow." *Guru* means "lama." *Manju* means "gentle." *Gosha* means "voice."[128] These four words of purpose are combined as

---

128. The Tibetan term for Manjushri is 'jam dbyangs, which literally means "gentle voice."

one. The [grammatical text entitled] *Kalapa* states, "That is addressed as YA, whereby it becomes endowed with life through YA. It possesses the sound of the syllable AH, making it a long [vowel]. Therefore the SHA [prior to the YA] is endowed with the life syllable AH, making the YA a long vowel, whereby it is GOSHA YA." [The entire phrase] means "I prostrate to Guru Manjushri" and is an expression of worship.

The Meaning of the Subject Matter of the Composition has two sections:

1. A Brief Explanation
2. An Extensive Explanation

A Brief Explanation

The first verse states:

> I and all beings equaling the extent of space
> Go for refuge until the essence of enlightenment [is reached]
> To the Buddhas, Dharma, and Sangha of the three times;
> Please liberate us from the fear of this life, the next life, and the
> bardo.

The first line reveals those who are going for refuge,[129] the second line reveals for how long you will go for refuge, the third line reveals the objects of refuge, and the fourth line reveals the fears from which you are seeking refuge. The Buddha jewel is the Sugatas of the three times of past, present, and future. As for calling the Buddhas *Sugatas*,[130] it is because they have gone to the ground endowed with three special qualities of the resultant bliss, abandonment, and realization through the blissful path. The term "Dharma" is used because the Dharma jewel has the two qualities of scripture and realization. The term "assembly" is used for the Sangha jewel because they are an assembly of superior[131] shravakas, pratyekabuddhas, and bodhisattvas. With respect to the person going

---

129. The sequence of the lines differs slightly in the English translation; therefore I have made the appropriate changes in the English translation of the commentary.
130. Tib. *bde bshegs*. This means "gone to bliss," or *Sugata* in Sanskrit.
131. Tib. *phags pa*. This refers to beings who have a direct realization of emptiness.

for refuge, this refers to yourself and all six classes of beings who equal the extent of space, together with those in the intermediate state. With respect to the time, since this is a Mahayana refuge, you are going for refuge until you attain the essence of enlightenment. For the essence of enlightenment, there is the truth body of exalted wisdom as the realization of the essence of enlightenment; the abode of the enjoyment body in the Gandavyuha realm of Akanishta as the essence of enlightenment; and the abode of the emanation body in Bodhgaya, India, as the essence of enlightenment.

With respect to the object of your fears from which you are seeking refuge, there are the fears of this life, the fears of your future lives, and the fears of the intermediate state of becoming. There aren't any fears that are not included in these three; therefore we are requesting liberation from these fears. It is these later ones that I will briefly present in this text.

Well then, it is not only the fears of the intermediate state that we are requesting liberation from but [the fears of] this life and the next as well.

Query: Then why is this text called "*Liberation from [Fear of] the Perilous Journey of the Intermediate State?*"

Response: In general, it is stated that just as when you burn one corner of a woolen cloth, you say that the woolen cloth is burnt, so it is not contradictory to the appearance of the whole to arrange the phrasing as either "referring to the collection as the parts," or "referring to the parts as the collection."[132] In particular, [Naropa's] *Clear Summary of the Five Stages*[133] states, "You should mix the three intermediate states." Thus there are (1) the intermediate state of birth and death between birth and death, (2) the intermediate state of dreams between going to sleep and awakening, and (3) the intermediate state of becoming between death and taking rebirth. Thus it is acceptable to assert that the fears of the intermediate state include all the fears of this life and the next.

---

132. The point being made here is that just as it is appropriate to say that a cloth is burnt when only a portion of it is burnt or to refer to a collection of items as constituting the parts of the item, in the same way, although the text is called *Liberation from [Fear of] the Perilous Journey of the Intermediate State*, the intention is to protect you from fears of this life and the next life as well.

133. Tib. *Rim lnga bsdus pa gsal ba*.

An Extensive Explanation

It is also perfectly acceptable to present either the three means of enlightenment through this life, the intermediate state, and rebirth, or to combine them into the respective practices done in this life, as you are approaching death, and in the intermediate state. However, in this text it is presented in two sections:

1. How to Condense the Essence of Practice for Your Whole Life
2. How to Practice the Mixings at the Time of Death

How to Condense the Essence of Practice for Your Whole Life has two sections:

1. How to Extract the Essence of [a Life of] Great Meaning
2. How to Stop Meaningless Distractions

How to Extract the Essence of [a Life of] Great Meaning

The second verse states,

> This excellent body is difficult to obtain and is easily destroyed;
> With it, we have the choice between profit and loss, happiness and suffering;
> Grant your blessing that we may extract its great meaning
> Without being distracted by the meaningless affairs of this life.

This life is difficult to find in terms of both cause and result. Although it is easy to be liberated from the fear of some minor condition, like a river of water, right now we have obtained an excellent support of this vajra body of leisure and endowments, with which we can easily accomplish all of our temporary and ultimate needs. If you give up your thoughts of this life and act in accordance with the Dharma, you will begin sowing the seeds of happiness and profit from it. [However,] if you accumulate nonvirtues for the sake of this life, you will begin sowing the seeds of suffering and will suffer a massive loss. You have the opportunity to decide which of these two you are going follow. Je Milarepa said, "Meritorious beings desire liberation with the great ship of this body of leisure and endowments, whereas wicked beings accumulate nonvirtues and are led to the lower realms. This is the demarcation line between progressing upward and declining downward. Oh my, this is an extremely important time, when we have the opportunity to choose between lasting happiness and lasting faults as our share of profit and loss." The great Yongzin Pandita also proclaimed, "You should consider this to be the demarcation line between progressing upward and declining downward. Right now you have complete choice for ultimate happiness." Therefore, do not let your mind be distracted by meaningless activities for the sake of this life alone, such as the awful actions of the eight [worldly concerns, or samsaric] dharmas of white, black, and variegated [actions] like subduing your enemies, protecting your loved ones, tending your cattle, and so forth. Instead, you are requesting, "Please grant your blessings that I may be able to extract the essence of this life of leisure and endowment and accomplish the great meaning of lasting happiness for myself and others."

As for how to extract the essence, Je [Tsongkhapa] himself stated, "The way to extract the essence [of this life] is to attain the state of enlightenment in one life by practicing the essence of the instructions of the supreme vehicle teachings in dependence upon the guru inseparable from the Buddha."

How to Stop Meaningless Distractions

The third verse states,

> We are separated from our possessions, all that we have accumulated is
>   exhausted,
> And at the end of rising comes descent, while
> Death is certain and the time of death is uncertain;
> Grant us your blessings that we may realize there is no time to waste.

Furthermore, the *Vinaya Scripture*[134] states,

---

134. Tib. *'Dul ba lung.*

> All accumulations end in being exhausted,
> The exalted ends in descent,
> Meeting ends in parting,
> Life ends in death.

A gathering where all your friends and acquaintances are gathered together at the same time must end in separation. Your possessions of food and wealth, which you have worked so hard for, are all exhausted in the end so that not even a sesame seed remains. Whatever lofty status you attain in samsara ends in decay and decline. The end of all that lives does not transcend death. Not only do you worry about death, but you have no idea when you are going to die; therefore, you should live as though you are going to die soon—such as today or tomorrow. Develop in your mental continuum the realization that there is no certainty as to the time of death; therefore, you have no time to waste accomplishing such meaningless activities of this life as tending to companions, wealth, clothing, and so forth. Therefore, you are requesting, "Please grant your blessings that I may extract the great value of this very moment through this teaching on death."

How to Practice the Mixings at the Time of Death has two sections:

1. Teaching the Means of Practicing the Rounds of Mixing
2. Teaching the Actual Way to Practice the Rounds of Mixing

Teaching the Means of Practicing the Rounds of Mixing has two sections:

1. Stopping Adverse Conditions to Practicing the Rounds of Mixing
2. Accomplishing Favorable Conditions for Practicing the Rounds of Mixing

Stopping Adverse Conditions to Practicing the Rounds of Mixing has two sections:

1. STOPPING THE SUFFERING ASSOCIATED WITH THE PAIN OF DEATH
2. STOPPING THE MISTAKEN APPEARANCES OF NONVIRTUE

Stopping the Suffering Associated with the Pain of Death

This is revealed in the verse that states,

> May we pacify the suffering of dying, when,
> In the city of mistaken conceptions of apprehended and
>   apprehender,
> The various causes of death are about to separate our
>   consciousness
> From our illusory aggregates composed of the four impure
>   elements.

The mental continuums of ordinary beings have conceptions of the external perceived object, such as forms, sounds, and so forth, and conceptions of the subjective mind, which envelops all phenomena in ignorance, whereby powerful, contaminated mistaken appearances emerge. In this way, from the perspective of such erroneous appearances, this great city of the three realms emerges. Whatever appears is not truly existent but is similar to illusory horses and elephants, and is produced from the thirty-six impure substances and the four elements as the various internal and external causes of death that are about to separate their four aggregates and mental consciousness. Therefore, you are requesting, "Grant your blessings that the violent sufferings from disturbing elements that cause the pain of death may be pacified and not occur."

With respect to the thirty-six impure elements, they are hair, nails, teeth, sweat, scent, flesh, bones, skin, channels, arteries, ducts, veins, heart, kidney, liver, spleen, intestines, lungs, colon, the upper part of the stomach, the lower part of the stomach, bladder, tears, saliva, mucus, feces, urine, lubricating fluids, marrow, fat, bile, pus, blood, lymph, brain, and nerves. As for the four elements, the flesh, bones, and so forth are the solid earth element; the blood, lymph, and so forth are the moist water element; the warmth of the upper and lower parts of the stomach are the increasing fire element; and the life-supporting wind and downward-voiding wind are the wind element of movement.

Regarding the instruction that describes "the causes of death,"[135] the "essential point" is explained in the explanatory tantra[136] that states,

> The essential points of infection are flesh, fat, and bone,
> And the essential bodily points are ligaments, internal organs, and
> veins.

Thus, whenever there is deterioration at the end of life, it is through either the essential points of the body or the essential points of illness. Regarding the causes of death, [Vasubandhu's] *Treasury of Abhidharma* states, "The end of life comes through water and so forth." Thus, once you have disturbed phlegm predominantly through the water element, disturbed bile predominantly through the fire element, or disturbed the wind predominantly through the wind element, your life is brought to an end through creating a deterioration of an essential point of the body.

As explained in [Je Tsongkhapa's] *Great Exposition on the Stages of the Path to Enlightenment*,[137] in every place of rebirth, with the exception of [the realms of] gods and hell beings,[138] your life will end in this way, and for a virtuous being there will be little harm to his [or her] life, whereas a nonvirtuous person will experience great harm to his [or her] life. If you are tormented by dying in that way, it will create obstacles for your practice of the mixings; therefore, you are requesting for that not to happen.

---

135. Tib. *gnad gcod*. This literally means "cutting the essential point," and refers to something that ends a life. Keep this in mind while reading the following sentences.

136. Tib. *bshad rgyud*. "Explanatory tantra" is a generic term that could refer to any number of explanatory tantras.

137. For a translation of this text, see Tsongkhapa, *The Great Treatise of the Stages of the Path to Enlightenment*, trans. Lamrim Chenmo Translation Committee (Ithaca, NY: Snow Lion Publications, 2000–2004).

138. This is because the gods and hell beings don't have bodies made of channels, winds, and drops that include the elements mentioned above.

Stopping the Mistaken Appearances of Nonvirtue

This is revealed in the verse that states,

> When we take our own lives with the weapons of the three
> poisons
> And the terrifying enemy—the Lord of Death—appears,
> We are deceived in our time of need by this body we have long
> since cherished;
> May we pacify these mistaken appearances of nonvirtue.

We cherish and care for our bodies through things such as food, clothing, a place to sleep, medical examinations, rituals, and so forth. Yet when we need our body most, it is useless, and we are deceived. [Shantideva's] *Guide to the Bodhisattva's Way of Life*[139] states,

> What need is there to mention complete torment
> When stricken with a terrifying illness, as
> I am seized by the physical apparitions of the
> Terrifying messengers of the Lord of Death?

The Lord of Death with his terrifying instruments is actually on his way to create impediments to your life and destroy you. Your mental continuum has a predominance of the three poisons as the afflictive emotions of attachment, anger, and ignorance. Accordingly, they appear as weapons of death as they come and take your own life. At that time, nonvirtuous beings perceive numerous horrifying shapes, as though in a dream, and they are overwhelmed with suffering and become filled with fear. Therefore you are requesting, "May I receive your blessings to pacify horrible mistaken appearances that are the result of such nonvirtues."

The explanatory tantra states,

---

139. Tib. *sPyod 'jug*. See Shantideva, *The Way of the Bodhisattva,* trans. Padmakara Translation Group (Boston: Shambhala Publications, 1997/2006).

> The three poisons of attachment, anger, and ignorance result
> in The faults of wind, bile, and phlegm.

From the three poisons come the three faults, and from those the three causes of death from wind, fire, and water are generated, whereby the weapons of the three poisons take your own life.

Accomplishing Favorable Conditions for Practicing the Rounds of Mixing has two sections:

1. Aspiring to Recall the Oral Instructions of Your Guru
2. Having Recalled Them, Aspiring to Gain a Degree of Confidence

Aspiring to Recall the Oral Instructions of Your Guru

This is revealed in the verse that states,

> When I am at a loss as to what I should do,
> The doctor has given up, rituals don't work,
> And my companions have abandoned their hopes for my life,
> May I recall the instructions of my guru.

The supreme conqueror, the Fifth Dalai Lama stated,

> When medicine, divinations, and rituals are of no benefit
> As you decline with each passing day,
> And companions, loved ones, and retinue have given up,
> This is the beckoning of the messengers of the Lord of Death.

Once the doctors have realized that you are not going to live and have abandoned their techniques, and although rituals are performed on your behalf, they cannot turn back the signs of death, [then] your living friends and loved ones will weep and, having decided you are not going to live, they will make preparations for your liturgy; some will be oppressed by suffering, and some will reveal an expression of great sadness. It is as though you are being destroyed by an enemy in the desert plains, and there is absolutely nothing you can do about it; you are ruined. Therefore, you are praying, "May I receive your blessings to be able to practice once I recall my guru's previous teachings, which provided oral instructions for me to contemplate and meditate on the three rounds of mixing [at the time of death]."

Having Recalled Them, Aspiring to Gain a Degree of Confidence

The next verse reveals your aspiration to gain a degree of confidence once you have recalled [your guru's instructions], when it states,

> May I be endowed with delight and confidence as
> Food and wealth accumulated through miserliness are left
>   behind,
> I am completely separated from my loving and longed-for
>   friends,
> And I go alone to that dreadful abode.

Gyalsay Rinpoche [Thogmey Zangpo (1297–1371)] stated,

> Wealth: you are supported by a hundred afflictive emotions when
>   searching for it;
> Once you find it, it is the foundation of miserliness while you
>   enjoy it;
> It is the cause of your lamenting if it is stolen by others,
> And is of no benefit once you die.

You are unable to give away your belongings because of miserliness, yet no matter how pleasing the food and wealth you have, you won't be able to take as much as your rice bowl with you, and you will go, leaving it all behind. Je [Tsongkhapa] himself said,

> In the midst of your loving companions,
> You must go on alone with extreme apprehension.

Through the force of your mutual love and affection for each other, you cannot bear to be separated even for an instant from those who have become your closest friends and loved ones, yet now you will be separated from them completely and will never meet them again. With great anxiety you must go alone without a companion through the long and perilous passageway of the intermediate state. It is at this time that the best Dharma practitioner will welcome death, a middling practitioner will have no fear, and the least will have no regrets. The great foremost being [Tsongkhapa] addressed the situation of the best practitioner when he said,

> In short, having realized the stimulus of my virtuous practice for recalling
> My previous meditation on bringing the three [bodies] into the path,
> Whenever death, the intermediate state, and rebirth arise,
> May I have an abundance of mental joy at the time of death.

Je [Tsongkhapa] also said,

> For ordinary birth, death, and the intermediate state,
> May I experience joyous delight through
> The three bodies of the Conqueror.

Thus you are requesting, "May I receive your blessings to attain a special mind of confidence at death through attaining mastery in the oral instructions for bringing the three bodies into the path with joyous delight, like a child returning home to his parents."

Teaching the Actual Way to Practice the Rounds of Mixing has three sections:

1. HOW TO PRACTICE THE ROUND OF MIXING DEATH WITH THE TRUTH BODY
2. HOW TO PRACTICE THE ROUND OF MIXING THE INTERMEDIATE STATE WITH THE ENJOYMENT BODY

3. How to Practice the Round of Mixing Rebirth with the Emanation Body

How to Practice the Round of Mixing Death with the Truth Body has two sections:

1. How to Practice during the Four Signs
2. How to Practice during the Four Empties

How to Practice during the Four Signs has two sections:

1. How to Practice during the First Three Signs
2. How to Practice during the Fourth Sign

How to Practice during the First Three Signs has two sections:

1. The Aspiration to Meditate on Bodhichitta Once You Have Recognized the External Signs
2. The Aspiration to Meditate on Emptiness Once You Have Recognized the Internal Signs

The Aspiration to Meditate on Bodhichitta Once You Have Recognized the External Signs

This is revealed in the verse that states,

> May I generate a powerful mind of virtue
> As the elements of earth, water, fire, and wind sequentially dissolve,
> The strength of my body is lost, my mouth and nose dry up and change,
> My warmth absorbs, and I gasp and cry out.

Aryadeva [third century CE] stated,

> The earth element dissolves into water;
> The water then dissolves into fire;
> The fire dissolves into the subtle element . . .

When you are dying, the earth, water, fire, and wind elements sequentially dissolve one into the other. With respect to their external signs, when earth dissolves into water and the strength of your body wanes, you are unable to move your limbs, you can't hold anything, and your body goes completely limp. You feel as though your body is sinking into the ground and you say, "Hold me up!" When the water element dissolves into the fire element, your mouth and nose dry out, your lower lip moves upward, and your tongue becomes short. When the fire element dissolves into the wind element, your bodily heat diminishes and finally collects into your heart. When signs such as these manifest, you should approach them with an extremely powerful virtuous mind, thinking, "For the welfare of all living beings I must actualize the state of the three bodies by transforming death into the truth body, the intermediate state into the enjoyment body, and rebirth into the emanation body," and pray, "Grant your blessings that I may be able generate the precious mind of bodhichitta." This is called "grasping and wailing." This is just a portion of the appearance of the four signs that will be explained below.

The Aspiration to Meditate on Emptiness Once You Have Recognized the Internal Signs

This is revealed in the verse that states,

> May I realize the natural state of immortality
> When the various mistaken terrifying appearances emerge,
> Especially as the mirage-, smoke-, and fireflies-like [appearances]
>   appear
> And the mount of the eighty natural conceptions ceases.

In accordance with the earlier explanation, when the elements dissolve, a nonvirtuous person experiences a variety of unpredictable and awful mistaken appearances that cause panic and terror. With respect to the particular internal signs, Mahasiddha Lawapa stated,

> First, there is an appearance like [a mirage for] a thirsty animal.
> The second sign is the appearance of smoke from a chimney.
> The third is similar to fireflies . . .

When the earth element dissolves into the water element, there emerges an appearance of an area being filled with water, similar to a mirage. When the water element dissolves into the fire element, there emerges a smoke-like appearance, similar to blue smoke billowing from a chimney. When the fire element dissolves into the wind element, there is an appearance similar to fireflies filling the sky, like a multitude of red sparks streaming upward.

There are thirty-three natural conceptions of white appearance:

> The three attachments and the three sorrows;
> Peace, conceptuality, and the three fears;
> The three cravings and grasping;
> Nonvirtue, hunger, thirst, and the three feelings;
> Cognizer, cognizing, and object cognized;
> Discrimination, shame, and compassion;
> The three affections and doubt;
> Collection and jealousy: these are the thirty-three.[140]

There are forty natural conceptions of red increase:

> Attachment, grasping, and the three joys,
> Rejoicing, rapture, amazement, and excitement;
> Contentment, embracing, kissing, and sucking;
> Stability, effort, pride, activity, and robbery;
> Force, delight, and the three engagements;[141]
> Vehemence, flirtation, and anger;
> Virtue, clear words and truth, and untruth;
> Definiteness and nongrasping;
> Benefactor, exhortation, and heroism;
> Nonshame, deceit, tightness, and viciousness;
> Nongentleness and dishonesty: [these] are the forty.

There are seven natural conceptions of black near-attainment:

---

140. This list is missing mental coming and going.
141. The three engagements are great, middling, and small nonvirtues performed out of pride.

Middling attachment, nonforgetfulness,
Mistakenness, nonspeaking, depression,
Laziness, and doubt: [these] are the seven.

When the winds that serve as the mounts of the eighty natural conceptions fully cease, it is conceptually imputed with the term "death"; therefore, you are praying, "Please grant your blessings that I may realize emptiness as the mode of existence of the not truly existent."

How to Practice during the Fourth Sign

This is revealed in the verse that states,

May I develop powerful mindfulness and introspection
As the wind element begins to dissolve into consciousness,
The outer flow of breath ceases, the coarse dualistic appearances
   dissolve,
And the appearance of a blazing butter lamp arises.

Aryadeva continues,[142]

. . . And wind dissolves into mind.

And Lawapa stated,

Fourth, there is clarity like a blazing lamp.

As the moving wind element of conceptual thought begins to dissolve into the mind of white appearance, the outer sign is that you gasp for air, have very long exhalations, and the death rattle begins. It is difficult to inhale, and although you do manage a little, it is short and rough. Finally, you exhale, and the inward and outward flow of the breath stops. Regarding the internal signs, once all other coarse conceptions of dualis-

142. This is the fourth line from the verse "The Aspiration to Meditate on Bodhichitta Once You Have Recognized the External Signs."

tic appearances of apprehender and apprehended dissolve, there manifests an appearance similar to a blazing candle that is undisturbed by wind. You are praying, "Grant your blessing that, at that time, I may generate very strong introspection conjoined with unwavering mindfulness that does not forget emptiness." With respect to the meaning of "the four signs dissolve into the four empties one after another," [Je Tsongkhapa's] *Lamp Perfectly Illuminating the Five Stages*[143] states, "After the power of the former is withdrawn, it becomes unclear, and it seems as though the power has shifted to the next one, whereby it is labeled with the phrase 'the former dissolved into the latter.'"[144]

How to Practice during the Four Empties has two sections:

1. How to Practice during the First Three Empties
2. How to Practice during the Fourth Empty

How to Practice during the First Three Empties

This is revealed in the verse that states,

> May I realize my own self-nature
> Through the yoga of realizing the emptiness of samsara and
> nirvana,
> As appearance, increase, and attainment dissolve one after the
> other,
> And the experience of moon, sun, and darkness emerge.

Aryadeva stated,

> The mental factors of the mind dissolve;
> The mental factors are ignorance.

---

143. Tib. *Rim lnga yang gsal sgron me*. The full title is *rGyud kyi rgyal pod pal gsang ba 'dus pa'i man ngag rim pa lnga pa rab tu gsal ba'i sgron me*. For a translation, see Tsongkhapa, *A Lamp to Illuminate the Five Stages: Teachings on Guhyasamaja Tantra*, trans. Gavin Kilty (Boston: Library of Tibetan Classics and Wisdom Publications, 2013).

144. This is referring to the dissolution of the four elements. Although the term "dissolved" is used to describe the sequential process, it is actually the case that as the strength of one element weakens, it becomes less apparent, making the others seem more apparent.

Once the minds of appearance, increase, and near-attainment dissolve one after the other, the experiences and realizations arise that are similar to an autumn sky pervaded by the moon, sun, and darkness. With respect to how this happens, as soon as the wind element completely[145] dissolves, the mind of appearance manifests and is vivid white, like a pure autumn sky pervaded by moonlight, extremely clear, luminous, and without a border. As soon as appearance dissolves into increase, the mind of increase manifests, which is like a pure autumn sky pervaded by sunlight that is vivid red or orange in appearance. During the upper portion of near-attainment, as near-attainment dissolves into increase, there is a pitch-black appearance, like a pure autumn sky during the first part of the night pervaded by darkness. Once you pass the demarcation line into the lower portion [of the mind of near-attainment], you are utterly without mindfulness and you pass into unconsciousness. However, this is not a fault because the stability of the forthcoming clear light depends on how long you remain in a state of unconsciousness. When such experiences arise, you should actualize your familiarity with the "sky yoga of emptiness," which realizes the empty reality of all phenomena of samsaric existence and the peace of nirvana. This accords with the advice of Changkya Rolpai Dorje [Rinpoche (1717–86)] that states,

There is no need to search; the seeker is within.

You are praying, "Grant your blessings that I may realize that all appearances are merely imputed by my mind and that my mind is also [the nature of] emptiness." This period is also revealed by the example of a rope discarded by an old man.

How to Practice during the Fourth Empty has two sections:

1. How to Manifest the All-Empty Clear Light
2. How to Conjoin That with Simultaneously Born Bliss

---

145. At this point it is important to recall that during the candle-flame-like appearance, the wind element had only partially dissolved into consciousness.

How to Manifest the All-Empty Clear Light

This is revealed in the verse that states,

> When I experience the autumn-like sky free from
> Pollutants and where all conceptual elaborations are pacified
> Through the dissolution of near-attainment into the all-empty
>   [clear light],
> May I have a meeting of the mother and son clear lights.

Aryadeva stated,

> Furthermore, progress toward the clear light.

Once you awaken from the lower section of near-attainment that lacks mindfulness, the "all-empty [clear light]" arises, and [this] is conventionally designated as "the near-attainment dissolves into the all-empty clear light." Therefore, having pacified all coarse and subtle obscuring conceptual elaborations without exception, the actual clear light dawns, which is like a pure autumn sky at dawn that is free from the three polluting conditions of moonlight, sunlight, and darkness that obscure the natural color of an empty sky. When that experience manifests, you are praying, "Grant your blessings that, once I conjoin that with my previous meditation on the pure view of emptiness, the mother and son clear lights may meet."

The clear light that naturally manifests during death, which is a pure vacuity like a pristine autumn sky, is the basic clear light and is called the "mother clear light." From the point when you perceive the all-empty clear light that you actualized previously through the methods of collecting the winds [into your central channel] onward, you seek the pure view of emptiness and meditate on the union of bliss and emptiness on the path clear light, and [this] is called the "son clear light"; therefore, the [meeting] of those two is "the meeting of the mother and son [clear lights]." Je Milarepa proclaimed, "The truth body is the clear light of death. That is what you should recognize. To be able to recognize that, you need to receive pointing-out instructions of the holy guru, which will enable you to understand the meaning of the view of the nature of reality and to train in the symbolic clear light of the path." We should realize [emptiness] in accordance with his instruction.

How to Conjoin That with Simultaneously Born Bliss

This is revealed by the verse that states,

> Through the melting of the moon by pure lightning-like fire,[146]
> May I abide in single-pointed absorption on the
> Exalted wisdom unifying simultaneously born bliss and
>   emptiness
> During the four empties.

The *Samputa Tantra* states,

> It is called lightning and is similar to light.

And,

> The Brahma fire at the point of the tri-juncture.

[The Hevajra Tantra in Two Chapters Entitled] "The Two Examinations" states,

> The rabbit bearer HAM drips through being scorched.

During the fourth empty—the all-empty clear light—the lightning follows and is called "the light of lightning," which is being compared to the Brahma fire at the navel and secret place. Its particles are the essence of inner fire and are the nature of the hot fire of red bodhichitta, which blazes upward and melts the white bodhichitta that is nominally imputed as the "rabbit bearer" and abides at the crown of your head. As it is collected into the red and white elements as the indestructible drop

---

146. What is being translated as "pure fire" is *tshang ba'i me* in Tibetan, which literally means "the Brahma fire," while the Tibetan term *ri bong can*, which literally means "rabbit bearer," is synonymous with the moon and is being translated as such. This is important to keep in mind during the following description

at your heart, you sequentially generate joy, supreme joy, extraordinary joy, and simultaneously born joy.[147] Through this, the object of experience is simultaneously born bliss, the appearing object is the all-empty clear light, and the apprehended object is emptiness as the absence of inherent existence of all phenomena. In that way, you conjoin bliss and emptiness as the truth body of exalted wisdom. Shridhara states,

> You should abide in the union of exalted wisdom
> In every session, a single day,
> A half month, month, year,
> Eon, or even a thousand eons.

Therefore you are praying, "Grant your blessing that I may be able to remain in single-pointed equipoise."

How to Practice the Round of Mixing the Intermediate State with the Enjoyment Body has three sections:

1. How the Best Person Mixes through the Force of Winds
2. How the Middling Person Mixes through the Force of Aspiration
3. How the Lesser Person Should Transform the Outer, Inner, and Secret

How the Best Person Mixes through the Force of Winds

This is revealed in the verse that states,

> When I arise from that state, may the mere wind and mind
> Of the clear light of death arise in the bardo;
> May I complete the illusory-like concentration as the complete
>   enjoyment body
> Blazing with splendor of the signs and indications.

---

147. For an explanation of this process, see Ngulchu Dharmabhadra and the Fifth Ling Rinpoche, *The Roar of Thunder*, p. 195.

The Omniscient Je [Tsongkhapa] stated,

> Through that stage, may I complete the illusory-like concentration
> As a web of magical emanation bodies
> Arises simultaneously from the example [clear light]
> Like fish arising from a crystalline river.

As explained above, once the signs emerge that you are stirring from that meditative equipoise, when you arise, the previous clear light of death is transformed. With the extremely subtle life-supporting wind that is the mount of the clear light functioning as the substantial cause and the mind of clear light functioning as the cooperative condition, as a substitute for the forthcoming intermediate state you imagine that you arise in the complete enjoyment body, ablaze with the glory and brilliance of the thirty-two noble signs and the eighty noble indications, while in reality you accomplish the illusory body of the third stage that is the illusory-like concentration. Therefore, you are praying, "Grant me your blessings that I may completely progress through these remaining stages." For this, there are both the actual illusory body and a similitude. When you actually accomplish it, you are able to actualize the result. If you don't accomplish more than a similitude, you must train in the round of mixing rebirth with the emanation body.

How the Middling Person Mixes through the Force of Aspiration

This is revealed in the verse that states,

> **If I must experience a bardo created by karma,**
> **May I immediately analyze birth, death, and the bardo,**
> **And once I realize the untrue existence of suffering,**
> **May I purify mistaken appearances.**

If you are incapable of arising in the illusory body and you accomplish an intermediate state of any of the six classes of living beings through the force of contaminated karma, without a moment's delay you should immediately implement perfect reasoning to examine and investigate it. The *Treasury of Abhidharma* states,

> Whoever is within samsara will experience
> Death and birth for as long as they exist.

Thus you are praying, "Once I realize that not even a [single] atom of [all] the terrors and sufferings of the intermediate state of existence that occur between conditioned birth and conditioned death is truly existent, please grant your blessing that I may transform all mistaken appearances of the environment and its beings so that all that appears may arise as pure deities and celestial mansions, [realize that] the deities' bodies are illusory, and [also realize that] the illusory is the nature of bliss and emptiness."

How the Lesser Person Should Transform the Outer, Inner, and Secret

This is revealed in the verse that states,

> When the various uncertain signs emerge, such as
> The four sounds of the reverse elements and the three fearful
>   appearances,
> May I be reborn in a pure land through the
> Outer, inner, and secret yogas of transformation.

Previously, the four elements of earth, water, fire, and wind dissolved in a forward progression. This verse is referring to when they are generated in reverse order, as the winds are stirred and emerge and the four terrifying sounds arise, such as a forest being incinerated by fire, the waves of an ocean being agitated, or a mountain being torn asunder and crashing down. There are terrifying appearances, such as your dwelling falling into three dreadful abysses: black for those with great anger, red for those with great attachment, and white for those with great ignorance. There are six uncertainties: (1) uncertainty of abode, (2) uncertainty of food, (3) uncertainty of clothes, (4) uncertainty of conduct, (5) uncertainty of mental appearances, and (6) uncertainty of companions. When you stabilize the various mistaken appearances that have arisen, you should recognize them as the intermediate state. Je Mitra Dzoki stated,

> You should transform the outer, inner, and secret.

The outer is transforming the appearance of the environment into a pure land, the inner is transforming the appearance of the inhabitants into the aspect of your personal deity, and the secret is the yoga of purifying the environment and its beings and transforming them into the display of bliss and emptiness through the force of yoga. Therefore you are praying, "Grant your blessing so that, through the force of this, I may take rebirth in a pure land of a buddha that is purified of the faults of existence, in a place such as Tushita, Sukhavati, and so forth."

How to Practice the Round of Mixing Rebirth with the Emanation Body

This is revealed by the verse that states,

> Please grant your blessings that I may assume a supreme
> Body as a knowledge holder in Kechara or
> The body of a celibate endowed with the three higher trainings,
> And once I perfect the realizations of the paths of the two stages,
> May I swiftly attain the three bodies.

The oral instructions state,

> If I do not accomplish the three bodies,
> May I become the principal knowledge holder
> And sequentially accomplish the [realization of] mahamudra.

The physical supports of practitioners of secret mantra can be classified as enjoying below the earth, enjoying upon the earth, and enjoying in the sky.[148] With respect to Kechara,[149] *Illumination of All Hidden Meaning*[150] states, "The dakas and dakinis with a special support for practicing mantra dwell in a unique abode in the sphere of space; therefore, the abode for engaging in the supreme practices of mantra is the abode of Kechara." In that way, there are also numerous stages in Kechara, of which the knowledge holder is supreme. Alternatively, you can intentionally take rebirth in a human body that is the supreme basis for practicing celibacy in a place similar to a central land in this world, as a fully ordained monk or nun endowed with completely pure three higher trainings of moral discipline, concentration, and wisdom. Therefore you are praying, "Grant your blessing that I may quickly attain without delay—in no more than one or two rebirths—the resultant truth body, enjoyment body, and emanation body once I perfect the experience and realization of sutra and tantra, or [in other words,] the two stages of generation and completion in that life." With respect to meditating on bringing rebirth into the path of the emanation body, there are two options: (1) you accomplish a similitude of the illusory body, or (2) you apprehend the intermediate state through the force of aspiration.[151]

The Meaning of the Conclusion of the Composition has three sections:

1. DESCRIBING THE COLOPHON
2. SECRET PRECEPTS
3. EXPLAINING THE ESSENTIAL POINTS OF PRACTICE

Describing the Colophon

Our text states,

---

148. For a detailed explanation of this, see Kyabje Trijang Rinpoche, *Ecstatic Dance of Chakrasamvara*.

149. Tib. *mKha' spyod*. This literally means "enjoying the sky."

150. Tib. *sBas don kun gsal*. This is Je Tsongkhapa's masterpiece commentary on the *Chakrasamvara Root Tantra*.

151. This is because in order to transform rebirth into the path of the emanation body during the actual process of death, you must be able to maintain some sense of awareness and divine pride during the intermediate state that precedes it.

> This completes the prayer entitled "A Supplication for
> Liberation from [Fear of] the Perilous Journey of the Inter-
> mediate State." It was composed solely as an encourage-
> ment for those earnest seekers by the Shakya monk Losang
> Chökyi Gyaltsen [the First Panchen Lama] in accordance
> with the sacred oral instructions of the sutras and tantras.
> It was composed in a room at the great monastic institu-
> tion glorious Drepung.

This reveals the composition, the earnest seekers, the composer, and the
abode, which are easy to understand.

Secret Precepts

Our text states, *"This should be kept secret from those who are unsuitable vessels and who have not received a highest-yoga-tantra empowerment."* This text
contains profound points of the completion stage; therefore if it is read
by someone who hasn't received a highest-yoga-tantra empowerment, it
becomes a root downfall, as stated by Bhawi when he declared,

> Proclaiming secrets to unripened
> Living beings is the seventh [root downfall].

Thus, it becomes a root downfall. To explain what happens if you explain
[tantra] to those who, although they have received an empowerment, are
without faith, Nagarjuna proclaimed,

> Teaching Dharma to those without faith.

Thus, it becomes a secondary downfall, and both the speaker and the
listener are damaged. The explanatory tantra *Vajramala*[152] states,

> If he perfectly bestows the empowerment he does not possess,
> Even though the practitioner may understand the meaning of
>   tantra,

---

152. Tib. *bShad rgyu rdo rje 'phreng ba.*

The master and disciple will equally go to
The great unbearable hell.

Explaining the Essential Points of Practice

Our text states,

> It is permissible to also supplement it by affixing a suppli-
> cation to your personal deity at the end. If you practice
> this while recalling the meaning, at the time of death you
> will become the king of the teachings.

The personal deity should be a highest-yoga-tantra deity, such as Guhyasamaja, Yamantaka, Heruka, or Hevajra. As for the term "supplication,"
the very best thing would be to perform the guru yoga supplications that
are a preliminary for the completion stage,[153] and supplement that with
numerous profound instructions for the time of death. The way to do this
should be learned by those with intelligence by analyzing the meaning of
the words.

COLOPHON

This completes the text *A Commentary on Liberation from Fear of the Perilous Journey of the Intermediate State Entitled "Adorning the True Intent of
the [First] Panchen [Lama]."* It was inspired by the writings of Tongnyi
Namkai Naljorpa and requested by the chant leader Yeshe Tsultrim. This
oral teaching was taught by the one bearing the name Losang, and was
inscribed by Shelkar Kalden Gyatso. I made a detailed analysis of my
guru's oral instructions and extracted the best sections; however, there
was no colophon [in his writings,] so I extracted the best parts. These
teachings were compiled by [myself, Ngulchu] Dharmabhadra. [This text]
was composed in Ngulchu Cave in the year of the bull, on an auspicious
day during the waxing moon of the third month.

---

153. For the preliminary ritual of guru yoga unique to the completion stage of Chakrasamvara composed by the First Panchen Lama, see Ngulchu Dharmabhadra and Panchen Chökyi
Gyaltsen, *The Source of Supreme Bliss.*

Outline of the Text

1. The Meaning of the Opening Line of the Composition (109–10)
2. The Meaning of the Subject Matter of the Composition (110–33)
3. The Meaning of the Conclusion of the Composition (133–35)

The Meaning of the Subject Matter of the Composition has two sections:
1. A Brief Explanation (110–11)
2. An Extensive Explanation (111–33)

An Extensive Explanation has two sections:
1. How to Condense the Essence of Practice for Your Whole Life (112–14)
2. How to Practice the Mixings at the Time of Death (114–33)

How to Condense the Essence of Practice for Your Whole Life has two sections:
1. How to Extract the Essence of [a Life of] Great Meaning (112–13)
2. How to Stop Meaningless Distractions (113–14)

How to Practice the Mixings at the Time of Death has two sections:
1. Teaching the Means of Practicing the Rounds of Mixing (114–20)
2. Teaching the Actual Way to Practice the Rounds of Mixing (120–33)

Teaching the Means of Practicing the Rounds of Mixing has two sections:
1. Stopping Adverse Conditions to Practicing the Rounds of Mixing (114–18)
2. Accomplishing Favorable Conditions for Practicing the Rounds of Mixing (118–20)

Stopping Adverse Conditions to Practicing the Rounds of Mixing has two sections:
1. Stopping the Suffering Associated with the Pain of Death (115–16)
2. Stopping the Mistaken Appearances of Nonvirtue (117–18)

Accomplishing Favorable Conditions for Practicing the Rounds of Mixing has two sections:
1. Aspiring to Recall the Oral Instructions of Your Guru (118–19)
2. Having Recalled Them, Aspiring to Gain a Degree of Confidence (119–20)

Teaching the Actual Way to Practice the Rounds of Mixing has three sections:
1. How to Practice the Round of Mixing Death with the Truth Body (121–29)
2. How to Practice the Round of Mixing the Intermediate State with the Enjoyment Body (129–32)
3. How to Practice the Round of Mixing Rebirth with the Emanation Body (132–33)

How to Practice the Round of Mixing Death with the Truth Body has two sections:
1. How to Practice during the Four Signs (121–25)
2. How to Practice during the Four Empties (125–29)

How to Practice during the Four Signs has two sections:
1. How to Practice during the First Three Signs (121–24)
2. How to Practice during the Fourth Sign (124–25)

How to Practice during the First Three Signs has two sections:
1. The Aspiration to Meditate on Bodhichitta Once You Have Recognized the External Signs (121–22)
2. The Aspiration to Meditate on Emptiness Once You Have Recognized the Internal Signs (122–24)

How to Practice during the Four Empties has two sections:
1. How to Practice during the First Three Empties (125–26)
2. How to Practice during the Fourth Empty (126–29)

How to Practice during the Fourth Empty has two sections:
1. How to Manifest the All-Empty Clear Light (127–28)
2. How to Conjoin That with Simultaneously Born Bliss (128–29)

How to Practice the Round of Mixing the Intermediate State with the Enjoyment Body has three sections:
1. How the Best Person Mixes through the Force of Winds (129–30)
2. How the Middling Person Mixes through the Force of Aspiration (130–31)
3. How the Lesser Person Should Transform the Outer, Inner, and Secret (131–32)

How to Practice the Round of Mixing Rebirth with the Emanation Body (132–33)

The Meaning of the Conclusion of the Composition has three sections:
1. Describing the Colophon (133–34)
2. Secret Precepts (134–35)
3. Explaining the Essential Points of Practice (135)

PART 3

Prayers and Supplications

Supplications to the Guiding Lineage Gurus of the Profound Path of the Six Yogas of Naropa

BY THE SEVENTH DALAI LAMA AND PABONGKHA RINPOCHE

My glorious and precious root guru:
Please sit on the lotus and moon at my crown,
Care for me with your great kindness,
And remain firm until the essence of enlightenment [is reached].[154]

I make requests to Heruka, the pervasive lord of the mandala of
    great bliss,
Jnanabhadra,[155] who perfected the realization of bliss and emptiness,
And Narotapa, the embodiment of Heruka;
Please bestow the exalted wisdom of bliss and emptiness.

I make requests to Marpa, the crown ornament of vajra holders,
Lord Milarepa, the laughing vajra who attained the vajra ground,
And Dakpo, the physician of the supreme vajra lineage;
Please bestow the exalted wisdom of bliss and emptiness.

I make requests to Phagmo Drukpa, the great protector of living
    beings,
Jigten Rinchen Gon, the guide of migrators,
And Rechung of Tsang, who perfected the welfare of living beings;
Please bestow the exalted wisdom of bliss and emptiness.

---

154. This prayer is based on a composition by the Seventh Dalai Lama, Kelsang Gyatso, with
amendments made by Pabongkha Rinpoche.
155. Tib. Shes rab bzang. This is another name for Tilopa (988–1069).

I make requests to Jampa Palwa, the lord of translators,
Sonam Wangpo, a treasury of Dharma linguistics,
And Sonam Sengé, the expounder of logic;
Please bestow the exalted wisdom of bliss and emptiness.

I make requests to Yangtsewa, who perceived the meaning of the
 scholars' scriptures,
Buton Rinchen Drup, the crown ornament of scholars,
And Jampa Palwa, the great scholar and siddha;
Please bestow the exalted wisdom of bliss and emptiness.

I make requests to Drakpa Jangchub with dharma eyes,
All-knowing Losang Drakpa, the king of the Dharma,
And his supreme Dharma son, Kädrup the Great;
Please bestow the exalted wisdom of bliss and emptiness.

I make requests to Jetsun Basowa, with perfect intellect,
Chökyi Dorje, who discovered complete liberation,
And Losang Dondrup, the great guide;
Please bestow the exalted wisdom of bliss and emptiness.

I make requests to Sangye Yeshe, destroyer of mistaken conceptions,
Losang Chökyi Gyaltsen, who perceives all things,
And Damchö Gyaltsen, the great ascetic;
Please bestow the exalted wisdom of bliss and emptiness.

I make requests to Menkhangpa, the lord of secret yogis,
To Nada Tsen, who actualized the good path of great secrets,
And Ngawang Jampa, the holder of a treasury of secrets;
Please bestow the exalted wisdom of bliss and emptiness.

I make requests to Yeshe Gyaltsen, the holy tutor,
To Ngawang Tenzin, the sovereign lord of the Buddha's complete
 teachings,
And to Yeshe Tenzin, thoroughly praised as the spiritual friend;
Please bestow the exalted wisdom of bliss and emptiness.

I make requests to Kelsang Tenzin, the great bodhisattva:
You are Manjushri Pada, the incarnation of all the conquerors,
Bearing the name Maitri, working to spread the
    profound meaning of the Conqueror's teachings;
Please bestow the exalted wisdom of bliss and emptiness.

I make requests to Chökyi Dorje, the skilled guide of beings:
Having perfectly realized the tantras' meaning of nondual method
    and wisdom,
You trained your mind with the essence of the profound path of
    method;
Please bestow the exalted wisdom of bliss and emptiness.

I make requests to Pema Dorje, the supreme siddha who reached
The final experience of the definitive meaning, practiced
    single-pointedly
In indefinite locations, and who reveals the path of definitive secrets;
Please bestow the exalted wisdom of bliss and emptiness.

Both of these previous verses were newly inserted by Pabongkha.

I make requests to my root guru, [Pabongkha] Dechen Nyingpo:
Your coarse and subtle channels and elements are the heroes, dakinis,
    and so on,
You are the embodiment of all the root and lineage gurus as the
    Three Jewels;
Please bestow the exalted wisdom of bliss and emptiness.

I make requests to Chakrasamvara, the pervasive lord of great joy,
The supreme Vajravarahi, who bestows the four joys,
And the heroes and dakinis, who are eternally delighted by joy;
Please bestow the exalted wisdom of bliss and emptiness.

Realizing that this life is as fleeting as a flash of lightning,
And that all the wonders of samsara must be abandoned,

Grant your blessings that I may direct my mind toward the Dharma
And generate renunciation and aversion for samsara.

For my welfare, my old mothers have undergone
Torments of body and mind in countless rebirths;
Grant me your blessing that I may generate compassion and bodhichitta,
Wishing to liberate them while striving in the conduct of a bodhisattva.

Grant me your blessings that I may always generate effortless
Faith and devotion for the kind lord, the root of all attainments,
And protect my commitments and vows just as I have promised
And cherish them as I do my life.

Grant me your blessings that I may ripen my mental continuum at
    this time
Through the realization of perceiving the nature of reality free
    from elaboration,
Seeing whatever appears as the mandala of the deity,
And mastering the experience of great bliss.

Grant your blessings that I may actualize the realization of
Simultaneously born bliss that comes from the touch of bodhichitta, as
A fresh wind[156] is generated through the outer and inner methods as
The winds enter the central channel and the inner fire blazes.

Grant your blessings that I may be able to accomplish whatever I desire
    without obstruction;
When the coarse winds and minds are free from activity, may sleep
Arise as the nature of the clear light of bliss and emptiness, and may I
Seize dreams and the bardo and transform them into emanations and so
    forth.

Grant your blessings that I may attain the magnificent clear light of
    simultaneously born bliss,

---

156. Tib. *dri gzhon gsar*.

Manifest the pure drops as the venerable father and mother,
Manifest a web of magical emanations,
And accomplish union in this life.

Grant your blessings that, should I have a karmic death,[157] at that time
I may develop a direct meeting of the mother and son clear lights,
Arise in the complete enjoyment body in the bardo,
And send forth emanations to guide living beings.

Grant your blessings that, through the concentration of phowa,
My mind may depart to the path of clouds through my crown to
    Kechara,
As well as accomplishing the yoga of entering the city of
Another's aggregates according to my wishes.

May I come under the loving care of glorious Heruka
Father and mother, as well as the dakinis of the three places,
Pacify the outer and inner obstructions, accomplish the favorable
    conditions,
And quickly perfect the path of the two stages.

SARVA MANGALAM

I make requests to the direct and indirect gurus,
Vajradhara, Tilopa, Naropa,
Marpa, Milarepa, Je Gampopa,
Phagmo Drukpa, and Gyalwa Drigungpa.

I make requests to my root guru, [Pabongkha] Dechen Nyingpo:
Your coarse and subtle channels and elements are the heroes, dakinis,
    and so on,

---

157. This means that you die before having achieved realizations high enough to transcend a death induced by your karma.

You are the embodiment of all the root and lineage gurus as the Three
Jewels;
Please bestow the exalted wisdom of bliss and emptiness.

Please grant your blessings that in this life I may generate
All the realizations and experiences of the glorious Six Yogas of Naropa,
Which is the supreme instruction, encapsulating one hundred thousand
Nectar streams of the profound essence of the father and mother
tantras.

*The publication of both the extensive and concise [prayers] to the lineage gurus of
the Six Yogas of Naropa was by sponsored by the sincere spiritual aspirant Gelong
Thubten Ngodrup.*

A Supplication for Liberation from [Fear of] the Perilous Journey of the Intermediate State Entitled "A Hero Liberated from Fear"

by The First Panchen Lama, Losang Chökyi Gyaltsen

NAMO GURU MANJUGOSHA

I and all beings equaling the extent of space
Go for refuge until the essence of enlightenment [is attained]
To the Buddhas, Dharma, and Sangha of the three times;
Please liberate us from the fear of this life, the next life, and the bardo.

This excellent body is difficult to obtain and is easily destroyed;
With it, we have the choice between profit and loss, happiness and
    suffering;
Grant your blessing that we may extract its great meaning
Without being distracted by the meaningless affairs of this life.

We are separated from our possessions, all that we have accumulated is
    exhausted,
And at the end of rising comes descent, while
Death is certain and the time of death is uncertain;
Grant us your blessings that we may realize there is no time to waste.

May we pacify the suffering of dying, when,
In the city of mistaken conceptions of apprehended and apprehender,
The various causes of death are about to separate our consciousness
From our illusory aggregates composed of the four impure elements.

When we take our own lives with the weapons of the three poisons
And the terrifying enemy—the Lord of Death—appears,
We are deceived in our time of need by this body we have long since
    cherished;
May we pacify these mistaken appearances of nonvirtue.

When I am at a loss as to what I should do,
The doctor has given up, rituals don't work,
And my companions have abandoned their hopes for my life,
May I recall the instructions of my guru.

May I be endowed with delight and confidence as
Food and wealth accumulated through miserliness are left behind,
I am completely separated from my loving and longed-for friends,
And I go alone to that dreadful abode.

May I generate a powerful mind of virtue
As the elements of earth, water, fire, and wind sequentially dissolve,
The strength of my body is lost, my mouth and nose dry up and change,
My warmth absorbs, and I gasp and cry out.

May I realize the natural state of immortality
When the various mistaken terrifying appearances emerge,
Especially as the mirage-, smoke-, and fireflies-like [appearances] appear
And the mount of the eighty natural conceptions ceases.

May I develop powerful mindfulness and introspection
As the wind element begins to dissolve into consciousness,
The outer flow of breath ceases, the coarse dualistic appearances
    dissolve,
And the appearance of a blazing butter lamp arises.

May I realize my own self-nature
Through the yoga of realizing the emptiness of samsara and nirvana,
As appearance, increase, and attainment dissolve one after the other
And the experience of moon, sun, and darkness emerge.

When I experience the autumn-like sky free from
Pollutants and where all conceptual elaborations are pacified
Through the dissolution of near-attainment into the all-empty
    [clear light],
May I have a meeting of the mother and son clear lights.

Through the melting of the moon by pure lightning-like fire,
May I abide in single-pointed absorption on the
Exalted wisdom unifying simultaneously born bliss and emptiness
During the four empties.

When I arise from that state, may the mere wind and mind
Of the clear light of death arise in the bardo;
May I complete the illusory-like concentration as the complete
    enjoyment body
Blazing with splendor of the signs and indications.

If I must experience a bardo created by karma,
May I immediately analyze birth, death, and the bardo,
And once I realize the untrue existence of suffering,
May I purify mistaken appearances.

When the various uncertain signs emerge, such as
The four sounds of the reverse elements and the three fearful
    appearances,
May I be reborn in a pure land through the
Outer, inner, and secret yogas of transformation.

Please grant your blessings that I may assume a supreme
Body as a knowledge holder in Kechara or
The body of a celibate endowed with the three higher trainings,
And once I perfect the realizations of the paths of the two stages,
May I swiftly attain the three bodies.

Colophon

This completes the prayer entitled *A Supplication for Liberation from [Fear of] the Perilous Journey of the Intermediate State*. It was composed solely as an encouragement for those earnest seekers by the Shakya monk Losang Chökyi Gyaltsen [the First Panchen Lama], in accordance with the sacred oral instructions of the sutras and tantras. It was composed in a room at the great monastic institution glorious Drepung. This should be kept secret from those who are unsuitable vessels and who have not received a highest-yoga-tantra empowerment. It is permissible to also supplement it by affixing a supplication to your personal deity at the end. If you practice this while recalling the meaning, at the time of death you will become the king of the teachings.

Glossary

Akshobya: Head of one of the five buddha families, he is blue in color and holds a vajra and bell. He is a physical representation of the purified aggregate of consciousness.

Amitabha: Head of one of the five buddha families, he is red in color and holds a lotus and bell. He is a physical representation of the purified aggregate of discrimination.

Basis, path, and result: Three points in time that are sequentially interrelated and transformed through a series of symbioses. The basis is our current body, speech, and mind, which function as the foundation. The path is the means of transforming those three states through spiritual practice. The result occurs when the mind becomes the truth body, the speech becomes the enjoyment body, and the body becomes the emanation body.

Bodhichitta: The intention to become enlightened for the welfare of all living beings, motivated by love and the compassion that sees the suffering nature of samsara and seeks to liberate all living beings from it.

Bodhisattva: An individual who has generated bodhichitta and has entered the path to enlightenment.

Buddha Shakyamuni: The historical Buddha, who lived approximately twenty-five hundred years ago and is the founder of Buddhism.

Channels: A channel is a passageway through which the winds and drops move. There are three primary channels: the central, right, and left. The ultimate goal of all highest-yoga-tantra practices is to bring the winds into the central channel and utilize the most subtle mind of clear light to realize the ultimate nature of reality.

Clear light: The extremely subtle mind that becomes manifest during the completion stage of highest yoga tantra and is utilized to realize emptiness.

Completion stage: The second stage of highest yoga tantra; utilizes channels, winds, and drops to cause the winds to enter, abide in, and dissolve into the central channel, whereby one manifests subtle levels of consciousness while conjoining them with bliss.

Daka: A male enlightened being who assists tantric practitioners to accomplish realizations of secret mantra.

Dakini: A female enlightened being who assists tantric practitioners to accomplish realizations of secret mantra.

Deity: There are both mundane and supramundane deities. A mundane deity is any god or goddess who has not attained either liberation or enlightenment. A supramundane deity is either a bodhisattva on one of the three final grounds or a buddha visualized in the aspect of a particular deity.

Dharma: The teachings of the Buddha, which lead one through spiritual paths that culminate in varying degrees of happiness, from the happiness of this life to the happiness of liberation and enlightenment.

Divine pride: The pride of being an enlightened being, which is generated by dissolving one's ordinary aggregates and their sense of identity and replacing it with the "divine" pride of being the deity. This entire process is utilized to strengthen one's realization of emptiness by realizing that the "I" is merely imputed.

Downward-voiding wind: See the entry for **root winds** below.

Drops: The drops are the subtle elements of the body that course through the channels within the body in dependence upon the movement of the inner energy that flows through the channels. The drops can be used to generate extraordinary blissful states of mind used to penetrate the nature of reality.

Emanation body: A coarse form body of an enlightened being that is emanated for the welfare of ordinary beings.

Empowerment (Tib. *dbang*): A ritual utilizing a mandala that transmits the blessing of a particular buddha in the aspect of a deity and establishes the imprints to attain the resultant body, speech, and mind of that deity.

Enjoyment body: The subtle body of an enlightened being that can be perceived only by bodhisattvas who have attained the path of seeing.

Five buddha families: Five buddhas that represent the five aggregates of an enlightened being— Akshobya as consciousness, Ratnasambhava as feeling, Amitabha as discrimination, Amoghasiddhi as compositional factors, and Vairochana as form.

Five stages of the completion stage: The natural sequence that occurs as a person gains progressively higher realizations of the completion stage: isolated speech, isolated mind, clear light, illusory body, and union.

Four empties: The four empties are (1) empty, (2) very empty, (3) great empty, and (4) all empty. They are synonymous with the four signs of white appearance, red increase, black near-attainment, and clear light, which are often referred to as the first, second, third, and fourth empty, respectively. They occur when the winds enter, abide in, and dissolve into the central channel through practice of the completion stage.

Four joys: Four increasingly blissful states of consciousness that are developed through melting the white drop at the crown. As the drop flows through the central channel from the crown to the throat, one develops joy; from the throat to the heart, one develops supreme joy; from the heart to the navel, one develops extraordinary joy; and when the white drop reaches the tip of the sex organ, one develops simultaneously born joy.

Four signs: The four signs of white appearance, red increase, black near-attainment, and clear light are often referred to as the first, second, third, and fourth empty, respectively. Alternatively, they are referred as empty, very empty, great empty, and all empty, respectively. They occur when the winds enter, abide in, and dissolve into the central channel through practice of the completion stage.

Generation stage: A term unique to highest yoga tantra, where one imagines transforming the basic experience of ordinary death, the intermediate state, and rebirth into the truth body, enjoyment body, and emanation body, respectively. Although there is self-generation as the deity in the lower classes of tantra, the lower tantras don't bring the three basic experiences into the path as the three bodies of a buddha.

Guhyasamaja: A highest-yoga-tantra deity who serves as a vehicle for actualizing our potential to reach the state of full enlightenment. Like all highest-yoga-tantra deities, Guhyasamaja contains two phases: generation and completion. Guhyasamaja practice is unique, however, in that being the first Buddhist tantra, its fives stages of the completion stage serve as a template for the vast majority of subsequent tantras.

Heroes and heroines: Male and female tantric deities who assist tantric practitioners to attain realizations.

Highest yoga tantra: The highest of the four classes of tantra, which emphasizes internal actions and utilizes embracing a physical consort as a means of generating the most subtle mind of clear light as a blissful subjective awareness capable of penetrating the nature of reality.

Illusory body: The subtle body that is actualized during the completion stage. There are two divisions of the illusory body: pure and impure. The impure illusory body is attained after the attainment of ultimate example clear light, and is so called because the wind from which it is composed is still impure in the sense that the mind from which it arose has yet to directly realize emptiness. The pure illusory body is so called because it arises from meaning clear light, which has directly realized emptiness.

Indestructible drop: The most subtle drop located within the heart channel wheel. It is composed of the essence of red and white drops obtained from the mother and father at the time of conception. It is also the abode of the most subtle mind of clear light that must be accessed to attain enlightenment.

Inner fire (Tib. *gtum mo*): Famous as "tummo meditation," inner fire refers to the subtle red element that is the nature of heat that resides within the navel channel wheel. Through causing the winds to enter, abide in, and dissolve into the central channel, the inner fire blazes and melts the white element at the crown, causing an extremely blissful and subtle level of mind that is unprecedented for its power to realize emptiness, the ultimate nature of reality.

Inner offering: There are two types of inner offering. The main inner offering contains a blessed pill called a "nectar pill," which is placed in a liquid, blessed, and offered to the guests. It is called the "inner offering" because the nectar pill is made of substances that represent the inner substances of living beings, and the same substances are visualized during the blessing of the inner offering itself. The second type is so called because the recipient is offered the inner tactile sense of an offering goddess.

Insertion of consciousness (Tib. *grong 'jug*): A rare and highly guarded practice in which a highly realized practitioner ejects his or her consciousness into a fresh corpse, thereby transferring his consciousness into that body, which is then used for the welfare of others, while the practitioner's old body is disposed of.

Intermediate state (Tib. *bar do*): The transitional state between the end of one life and the beginning of the next. The intermediate state can last up to forty-nine days and consists of seven minor transitional periods, each resulting in a "small death," after which one either takes rebirth or assumes another intermediate state body.

Isolated body: A preliminary to the five stages of the completion stage of Guhyasamaja as presented by Nagarjuna. It is so named because the wind that gives rise to the body as being ordinary is isolated from its movement by dissolving it into the central channel, which gives rise to the pure conceptions of the body as being the deity body.

Isolated mind: The second of the five stages of the completion stage of Guhyasamaja as presented by Nagarjuna. It is so named because the wind that gives rise to the mind as being ordinary is isolated from its movement by dissolving it into the central channel, which gives rise to the pure conceptions of the mind as being the deity's mind.

Isolated speech: The first of the five stages of the completion stage of Guhyasamaja as presented by Nagarjuna. It is so named because the wind that gives rise to the speech as being ordinary is isolated from its movement by dissolving it into the central channel, which gives rise to the pure conceptions of the speech as being the deity's speech.

Karma: The cause-and-effect relationship between an action and its corresponding result; whatever we experience is a result of our previous actions. Pleasant experiences stem from virtuous actions and painful experiences stem from nonvirtuous actions.

Karma mudra: A physical consort utilized to actualize the most subtle mind of clear light through completion-stage techniques of highest yoga tantra.

Lamrim: A Tibetan term in which *lam* means "path" and implies that it is a path to enlightenment; *rim* simply means "stages." Therefore, lamrim means "stages on the path to enlightenment." It is a term coined by Atisha in reference to his seminal text *A Lamp on the Path to Enlightenment*, and is now used to refer to the whole genre of material that maps out the entire path to enlightenment, from the initial entry up to the attainment of full enlightenment.

Life-supporting wind: See the entry for **root winds** below.

Madhyamaka: The "Middle Way" school of Mahayana philosophy founded by Nagarjuna. There are two primary divisions of the Madhyamaka: the Prasangika and the Svatantrika. The Prasangika utilizes consequential syllogisms and presents a slightly subtler interpretation of emptiness than does the Svatantrika. The Svatantrika utilizes autonomous syllogisms and presents emptiness in a slightly coarser interpretation than does the Prasangika.

Mahasiddhas: Tantric adepts who have attained varying degrees of realization far beyond that of an ordinary being. They are most often associated with ancient India.

Mantra: In the interpretive sense, a mantra is a set sequence of syllables used to invoke the blessings of a particular deity. In the definitive sense, a mantra is the audible expression of the particular qualities of an enlightened being's mind of bliss and emptiness.

Milarepa: Tibet's most famous yogi, Milarepa (1052–1135) spent the early part of his life engaged in nonvirtuous actions, eventually killing thirty-six people through the use of black magic. Repenting of his nonvirtuous actions, he sought out his guru, Marpa Chökyi Lodro (1012–97), who famously put him through extreme hardships as a means of purifying Milarepa's negative karma. Milarepa devoted the latter part of his life to solitary retreat, eventually attaining enlightenment and establishing numerous disciples on the path to enlightenment. His teachings were adopted by his disciple Gampopa Sonam Rinchen (1079–1153), who combined them with the teachings of Kadam lineage, which resulted in the Kagyu lineage.

Nada: A small, three-curved line that sits at the uppermost position of the syllable BAM and represents the three subtle minds of white appearance, red increase, and black near-attainment.

Nagarjuna: The founder of the Madhyamaka school of Mahayana Buddhism, Nagarjuna (c. 2nd century CE) is said to have traveled to the subterranean land of the nagas to obtain the perfection of wisdom sutras. (A naga is a serpent-like being that has varying degrees of power and can be either malevolent or benign.)

Naropa: One of the greatest tantric practitioners of India, Naropa's (1016–1100) guru was Tilopa (988–1069) and his foremost Tibetan disciple was Marpa Chökyi Lodro (1012–97). Naropa's most famous teaching is the Six Yogas of Naropa, which became the most widely used system of completion-stage practices in Tibet.

Outer offering: A ritual offering consisting of various "outer" substances, such as water, flowers, incense, and so forth.

Pervasive wind: See the entry for **root winds** below.

Phenomena source: Either a single or double tetrahedron that is used in Vajrayogini practice and that symbolizes, among other things, emptiness, and represents emptiness as the source of all phenomena.

Ratnasambhava. Head of one of the five buddha families, he is yellow in color and holds a jewel and bell. He is a physical representation of the purified aggregate of feeling.

Renunciation (Tib. *nges 'byung*): Literally, "definite emergence"; refers to the definite determination to be liberated, or emerge from samsara through a proper understanding of its shortcomings.

Root downfall: A violation of one of the root vows associated with either the pratimoksha, bodhisattva, or tantric codes of discipline. (Pratimoksha vows are a set of vows taken by Mahayana Buddhists with the motivation of attaining liberation from samsara.)

Root winds: The five winds that support various bodily functions and are the basis of the five buddha families: (1) the life-supporting wind, (2) the upward-moving wind, (3) the pervasive wind, (4) the equally abiding wind, and (5) the downward-voiding wind. These five winds dwell at (1) the heart chakra, (2) the throat chakra, (3) throughout the body, (4) the navel chakra, and (5) the secret chakra, respectively.

Samsara: A cycle of uncontrolled rebirth through the force of afflicted actions and delusions.

Seven-limbed prayer: As its name implies, the seven-limbed prayer contains seven parts: prostrating, offering, confessing, rejoicing, requesting the field of merit (i.e., the buddhas and bodhisattvas) to teach, beseeching them not to pass away, and dedication of merit. It is the most widely used means of accomplishing three of the most important components on the path to enlightenment: purification of negative karma, accumulation of merit, and receiving blessings.

Shabgyu: The "u" vowel in the Tibetan alphabet. It is hook shaped and can be affixed to the bottom of any letter, transforming it into a syllable.

Sutra: Discourses given by the historical Buddha.

Three bodies of a buddha: The truth body, the enjoyment body, and the emanation body. See the entry for **generation stage** above.

Transference of consciousness (Tib. *'pho ba*; Skt. *phowa*): A method to intentionally separate the subtle wind and mind from the coarse aggregates at the time of death as a means of taking rebirth in a pure land of a buddha.

Truth body (Skt. *dharmakaya*): The extremely subtle mind of an enlightened being that is completely free from the obstructions to omniscience and that serves as the foundation for the enjoyment and emanation bodies.

Tsok offering (Skt. *ganachakra*): A tantric feast involving ritual music and sacred substances for invoking the blessings of the dakas and dakinis and strengthening one's tantric commitments.

Tsongkhapa: A Tibetan lama responsible for the formation of the Gelug tradition of Tibetan Buddhism, Tsongkhapa (1357–1419) was a great nonsectarian teacher who assembled various practices and lineages that resulted in the Gelug tradition.

Ultimate reality: The ultimate reality of all phenomena is their being empty of inherent existence.

Union: There are several types of union: (1) the union of bliss and emptiness at either the generation or completion stage—most notably the latter, (2) the union of the illusory body and clear light, (3) the union of learning, and (4) the union of no-more-learning. The third one is synonymous with the union of the pure illusory body and meaning clear light, and the fourth is synonymous with enlightenment.

Upward-moving wind: See the entry for **root winds** above.

Vairochana: Head of one of the five buddha families, he is white in color and holds a wheel and bell. He is a physical representation of the purified aggregate of form.

Vajradhara: An emanation of Buddha Shakyamuni who appeared as a blue-colored deity and taught the various tantras.

Vajradharma: An aspect of Buddha Amitabha that is equivalent to Vajradhara and serves as the basis upon which a Vajrayogini practitioner identifies his or her spiritual guide.

Vajrasattva: A white-colored deity who is the embodiment of the purification powers of all enlightened beings.

Vajrayogini: A female enlightened being who is both the consort of Chakrasamvara and a tantric deity in her own right. Her practice is very simple yet profound and contains many unique instructions for attaining enlightenment in one life as well as for traveling to Kechara pure land.

Winds: There are coarse, subtle, and very subtle internal winds that are associated with human beings. The coarsest wind is our breath. The subtle wind functions to allow the movement of drops—or vital essences—within our body. The very subtle wind is inseparable from our very subtle mind, which ultimately transforms into the truth body and the enjoyment body, respectively.

Wisdom mudra: A visualized consort used in lieu of an actual consort as a means of developing a blissful subjective mind that is then used to ascertain emptiness.

Yoga tantra: The third of the four classes of tantra, yoga tantra places primary emphasis upon internal actions and utilizes holding hands with a physical consort as a means of generating a blissful subjective awareness used to penetrate the nature of reality.

Bibliography

Works in English

Aryadeva and Gyel-tsap. *Yogic Deeds of a Bodhisattva: Gyel-tsap on Aryadeva's Four Hundred*. Commentary by Geshe Sonam Rinchen. Translated by Ruth Sonam. Ithaca, NY: Snow Lion Publications, 1994. (Reprinted as Aryadeva and Gyel-tsap, *Aryadeva's Four Hundred Stanzas on the Middle Way: With Commentary by Gyeltsap*. Ithaca, NY: Snow Lion Publications, 2008.)

The Chakrasamvara Root Tantra. Translated by David Gonsalez. Somerville, MA: Wisdom Publications, 2020.

Chöden Rinpoche. *Stairway to the State of Union: A Collection of Teachings on Secret Mantra*. Translated and edited by Ian Coghlan and Voula Zarpani. Churchill, AU: Awakening Vajra Publications, 2012.

Gray, David B., trans. *The Chakrasamvara Tantra (The Discourse of Sri Heruka): A Study and Annotated Translation*. Treasury of the Buddhist Sciences. Somerville, MA: Wisdom Publications, 2019.

Hopkins, Jeffrey. *Meditation on Emptiness*. Boston: Wisdom Publications, 1983, 1996.

Kachen Yeshe Gyaltsen. *Manjushri's Innermost Secret: A Profound Commentary of Oral Instructions on the Practice of Lama Chöpa*. Translated by David Gonsalez. Somerville, MA: Wisdom Publications, 2019.

Kyabje Trijang Rinpoche Losang Yeshe. *The Ecstatic Dance of Chakrasamvara: Heruka Body Mandala Practice and Commentary*. Translated by David Gonsalez. Seattle: Dechen Ling Press, 2013.

Newland, Guy. *Appearance and Reality: The Two Truths in the Four Buddhist Tenet Systems.* Ithaca, NY: Snow Lion Publications, 1999.

————. *The Two Truths in the Mādhyamika Philosophy of the Ge-luk-ba Order of Tibetan Buddhism.* Ithaca, NY: Snow Lion Publications, 1992.

Ngulchu Dharmabhadra and the Fifth Ling Rinpoche Losang Lungtog Tenzin Trinley. *The Roar of Thunder: Yamantaka Practice and Commentary.* Translated by David Gonsalez. Somerville, MA: Wisdom Publications, 2021.

Ngulchu Dharmabhadra and the First Panchen Lama, Losang Chökyi Gyaltsen. *The Source of Supreme Bliss: Heruka Chakrasamvara Five Deity Practice and Commentary.* Translated by David Gonsalez. Somerville, MA: Wisdom Publications, 2022.

Pabongkha Dechen Nyingpo. *The Extremely Secret Dakini of Naropa: Vajrayogini Practice and Commentary.* Translated by David Gonsalez. Somerville, MA: Wisdom Publications, 2020.

————. *The Secret Revelations of Chittamani Tara: Generation and Completion Stage Practice and Commentary.* Somerville, MA: Wisdom Publications, 2023.

Shantideva. *The Way of the Bodhisattva.* Translated by the Padmakara Translation Group. Boston: Shamabhala Publications, 1997; revised edition, 2006.

Sterns, Cyrus, trans. and ed. *Taking the Result as the Path: Core Teachings of the Sakya Lamdré Tradition.* Library of Tibetan Classics, vol. 4. Boston: Wisdom Publications, 2006.

Tenzin Gyatso, the Fourteenth Dalai Lama. *Advice on Dying: And Living a Better Life.* Translated and edited by Jeffrey Hopkins. New York: Atria Books, 2002.

————. *The Gelug/Kagyü Tradition of Mahamudra.* Translated by Alexander Berzin. Ithaca, NY: Snow Lion Publications, 1997.

————. *The Union of Bliss and Emptiness: Teachings on the Practice of Guru Yoga.* Translated by Thupten Jinpa. Ithaca, NY: Snow Lion Publications, 2009.

Tsongkhapa [Tsong-kha-pa]. *The Great Treatise on the Stages of the Path to Enlightenment.* 3 vols. Translated by Lamrim Chenmo Translation Committee. Ithaca, NY: Snow Lion Publications, 2000–2004.

———— [Tsongkhapa]. *A Lamp to Illuminate the Five Stages: Teachings on*

Guhyasamaja Tantra. Translated by Gavin Kilty. Library of Tibetan Classics, vol. 15. Boston: Wisdom Publications, 2013.

———— [Tsongkhapa Lobzang Drakpa]. *Tsongkhapa's Six Yogas of Naropa*. Translated, edited, and introduced by Glenn H. Mullin. Ithaca, NY: Snow Lion Publications, 1996.

Tibetan Texts

Losang Chökyi Gyaltsen (blo bzang chos kyi rgyal mtshan) [The First Panchen Lama]. *A Supplication for Liberation from [Fear of] the Perilous Journey of the Intermediate State Entitled "A Hero Liberated from Fear" (Bar do 'phrang sgrol gyi gsol 'debs 'jigs sgrol gyi dpa' bo)*. In gSung 'bum blo bzang chos kyi rgyal mtshan, vol. 5, 73–76. New Delhi: Mongolian Lama Guru Deva, 1973. http://purl.bdrc.io/resource/MW23430_443AD1

Ngulchu Dharmabhadra (dngul chu d+harma b+ha dra). *A Commentary on Liberation from Fear of the Perilous Journey of the Intermediate State Entitled "Adorning the True Intent of the [First] Panchen [Lama]" (Bar do 'phrang sgrol gyi gsol 'debs 'jigs sgrol gyi dpa' bo'i rnam bshad pan chen dgongs rgyan)*. In gSung 'bum/ d+harma b+hadra (BDRC W6493), vol. 3, 379–406. Dngul Chu Bla Brang, 2000[?]. http://purl.bdrc.io/resource/MW6493

————. *Lecture Notes on the Six Yogas of Naropa, Entitled "Adorning the True Intent of the [Three] Inspirations" (Na ro chos drug gi zin bris yid ches dgongs rgyan)*. In gSung 'bum/ d+harma b+hadra (BDRC W6493), vol. 6, 845–934. Dngul Chu Bla Brang, 2000[?]. http://purl.bdrc.io/resource/MW6493

Tsongkhapa Losang Drakpa (tsong kha pa blo bzang grags pa). *A Sequential Guide to the Profound Path of the Six Dharmas of Naropa Entitled "Endowed with the Three Inspirations" (Zab lam na ro'i chos drug gi sgo nas 'khrid pa'i rim pa yid ches gsum ldan zhes bya ba)*. In rJe tsong kha pa'i gsung 'bum (BDRC MW29193), vol. 9, 5–128. Dharamsala: Sherig Parkhang, 1997. http://purl.bdrc.io/resource/MW29193_4C1B85

Index

The Dechen Ling Practice Series

Manjushri's Innermost Secret
A Profound Commentary of Oral Instructions on the Practice of Lama Chöpa
Kachen Yeshe Gyaltsen
Foreword by Ganden Tripa Lobsang Tenzin
Now available from Wisdom Publications

The Essence of the Vast and Profound
A Commentary on Je Tsongkhapa's Middle-Length Treatise on the Stages of the Path to Enlightenment
Pabongkha Rinpoche
Now available from Wisdom Publications

The Extremely Secret Dakini of Naropa
Vajrayogini Practice and Commentary
Pabongkha Rinpoche
Now available from Wisdom Publications

The Chakrasamvara Root Tantra
The Speech of Glorious Heruka
Now available from Wisdom Publications

The Roar of Thunder
Yamantaka Practice and Commentary
Ngulchu Dharmabhadra
and the Fifth Ling Rinpoche, Losang Lungtog Tenzin Trinley
Now available from Wisdom Publications

The Source of Supreme Bliss
Heruka Chakrasamvara Five Deity Practice
Ngulchu Dharmabhadra
and the First Panchen Lama, Losang Chökyi Gyaltsen
Now available from Wisdom Publications

The Secret Revelations of Chittamani Tara
Generation and Completion Stage Practice and Commentary
Pabongkha Rinpoche
Now available from Wisdom Publications

The Blazing Inner Fire of Bliss and Emptiness
An Experiential Commentary on the Practice of the Six Yogas of Naropa
Ngulchu Dharmabhadra
Now available from Wisdom Publications

The Melodious Drum of Dakini Land
A Commentary to the Extensive Dedication Prayer of Venerable Vajrayogini
Yangchen Drupay Dorje

Healing Nectar of Immortality
White Tara Healing and Longevity Practices and Commentary
Trijang Rinpoche and Aku Sherab Gyatso

The Ecstatic Dance of Chakrasamvara
Heruka Body Mandala Practice and Commentary
Trijang Rinpoche
Foreword by Gen Lobsang Choephel

About Wisdom Publications

Wisdom Publications is the leading publisher of classic and contemporary Buddhist books and practical works on mindfulness. To learn more about us or to explore our other books, please visit our website at wisdomexperience.org or contact us at the address below.

Wisdom Publications
132 Perry Street
New York, NY 10014 USA

We are a 501(c)(3) organization, and donations in support of our mission are tax deductible.

Wisdom Publications is affiliated with the Foundation for the Preservation of the Mahayana Tradition (FPMT).